SOUTHERN COOKING DONE LIGHT

SOUTHERN COOKING DONE LIGHT

Healthy Cooking Never Tasted So Good!

Frances F. Campbell

iUniverse, Inc.
New York Lincoln Shanghai

SOUTHERN COOKING DONE LIGHT
Healthy Cooking Never Tasted So Good!

Copyright © 2006 by Frances F. Campbell

All rights reserved. No part of this book may be used or reproduced by any means, graphic, electronic, or mechanical, including photocopying, recording, taping or by any information storage retrieval system without the written permission of the publisher except in the case of brief quotations embodied in critical articles and reviews.

iUniverse books may be ordered through booksellers or by contacting:

iUniverse
2021 Pine Lake Road, Suite 100
Lincoln, NE 68512
www.iuniverse.com
1-800-Authors (1-800-288-4677)

ISBN-13: 978-0-595-41565-6 (pbk)
ISBN-13: 978-0-595-85911-5 (ebk)
ISBN-10: 0-595-41565-2 (pbk)
ISBN-10: 0-595-85911-9 (ebk)

Printed in the United States of America

I dedicate this book in loving memory to my Father, Earl Ferguson.
Who died at age 49 from diabetes and heart trouble.
And
To my Husband, Bill Campbell,
Who died at the age of 52 from diabetes and heart trouble.

Contents

Introduction xi
My Favorite Brands xiii
Appetizers 1
Soups 10
Salads 17
Vegetables 28
Meats 47
Deserts 76
Breads 120
Muffins 131
Beverages 136
Successful Cooking Tips 139
A Note about Splenda 141
About the Author..143
Index 145

Acknowledgement

I would like to thank my daughter Charaman for all the time she spent helping me with this book. I also want to thank my son, Billy for his great ideas and encouragement.

Introduction

People always said my Mother was a good cook and of course I always thought they were right.

I was the youngest of two girls. I always wanted to help in the kitchen like my big sister but the only thing they would let me do was cut up vegetables. So, needless to say I never learned the secrets of my Mother's cooking until I was much older. In 1952, I married the love of my life Bill Campbell, he was in the U.S. Navy. So while, my husband was out at sea, I stayed with my parents and I learned to cook like Mother.

When I learned to cook we had never heard of high cholesterol or even high blood pressure. We knew about diabetes because my father was a diabetic but the only artificial sweetener at the time was saccharin. So when I learned to cook we used real butter, shortening, and sugar. No one ever knew the damages these could cause.

When my husband was diagnosed with diabetes in 1970, I wasn't quite sure what to do. How was I suppose to cook for a diabetic. My father was a diabetic but all he did was limit his sugar in take and very little at that. So, I was at a loss of what and how to cook. I tried making subtle changes in the way I cooked. I substituted beef bouillon cubes in things I would have used fat back in and stewed squash instead of frying. Some things turned out o.k. and others didn't. Trying to cook with artificial sweeteners in the 70's was disastrous. Splenda hadn't been invented yet and there were still very few sugar free items on the market. There was a sugar free gelatin on the market but not as good as what we have now. To make it taste better we would take what ever flavor the gelatin was and find a diet drink in the same flavor. Boil a cup of the soda pour it in the gelatin to dissolve it and then pour a cool cup of the soda in it. It made it taste much better. The only whip cream was the kind you beat with a mixer. Occasionally, you might find some sugar free ice cream and sugar free candy and cookies but nothing like what we have today. My husband dealt with it until his death in 1984. My daughter developed diabetes in 1996. She was a different story from my husband that dealt with it. She let me know if it didn't taste good she would not eat it. She loved chocolate and sweets and still does. I knew when she said she wasn't going to eat it if it didn't taste good she wasn't going to eat it. So, I embarked on a mission to change the Southern food we love from fatting to light. The result of my mission is this book. The fat and sugars have been taken out of the old southern recipes we loved but the newer healthy version we love just as much. I hope you enjoy the recipes in this book as much as I and my family have. Remember Healthy Cooking Never Tasted So Good.

My Favorite Brands

There are lots of good products on the grocery shelves today but these are my favorites. I feel these products are healthier, tastier, easy to get and deliver the most flavor for the least amount of fat, sugar or calories.

Carnation Evaporated skim milk

Mayfield milk, skim, 2% and 1%

Philadelphia Cream Cheese, Light

Kraft Light Mayonnaise

Kraft Light Salad Dressing

I Can't Believe Its Not Butter, Light

Pam cooking spray

Cool Whip Topping, Sugar Free

Splenda and Splenda blend

Jell-O sugar free gelatin and pudding

Bisquick Reduced Fat baking mix

Kraft 2% milk cheese

Peter Pan Reduced Fat Peanut butter

Appetizers

Fresh Fruit Dip

½ cup light mayonnaise
½ cup fat free sour cream
1/3 cup sugar free orange marmalade
1 tablespoon of 2% milk
Assorted fruit

In a small bowl, whisk mayonnaise, sour cream, marmalade and milk. Refrigerate until ready for serving. Served with assorted fruit.

Deviled Eggs

My daughter loves deviled eggs and this is her favorite recipe for them.

12 hard-boil eggs
¼ cup light mayonnaise
3-tablespoon chili sauce
1 teaspoon of mustard

Slice eggs in half scooping out yellows. Mix with Mayonnaise, chili sauce and mustard. Spoon back into egg whites. Sprinkle with paprika, bacon bits and cheese. Chill until served.

Cream Cheese Spread

12 Cherries
1 teaspoon Grated Orange Zest
1–8oz. Package Light Cream Cheese

Stir chopped pitted cherries and grated orange zest into whipped light cream cheese. Spread over crackers or bagels.

Banana Pops

6 Bananas
½ cup low calorie creamy peanut butter
1-cup miniature chocolate chips
12 Wooden Craft sticks

Peal bananas and cut each banana in half and insert a craft stick into each banana half. Place chocolate chips in a shallow bowl. Cover the banana with peanut butter then roll the banana in the chips. Freeze for 1 hour or until frozen.
Makes 12 pops

Peanut Butter Apple Dip

1–8 ounce package of fat free cream cheese softened
1 cup reduced fat peanut butter
1 cup brown splenda
¼ cup of 2% milk
Apples cut into wedges

In a mixing bowl combine the first four ingredients and mix well. Serve with apple wedges.

Store any left overs in refrigerator
Makes 2 2/3 cups

Chicken Livers and Bacon

1 carton of chicken livers
1 pound of bacon

Preheat oven to 350 degrees. Wrap each liver with a strip of bacon and secure with a toothpick. Place in shallow pan spray with non-stick spray and bake for 10 minutes turn once and bake 25 minutes drain on a paper towel and serve immediately.

Chocolate Fruit Dip

1–8 ounce package fat free cream cheese softened
1/3 cup Splenda
1/3 cup baking cocoa
1 teaspoon of vanilla extract
2 cups light cool whip
Assorted fruit for dipping

In a mixing bowl beat the cream cheese and splenda until smooth. Add cocoa and vanilla mix well. Beat in cool whip until smooth. Serve with fruit
Makes 2 cups

Sausage Balls

I serve these sausage balls every Christmas for my family. They love them.

1 pound of hot bulk sausage
2 cups of 2% milk extra sharp grated cheese
3 cups of reduced fat bisquick
1–3 tablespoons of skim milk

Mix first three ingredients and add milk one tablespoon at a time until well mixed. Form into 1-inch balls and bake at 350 degrees for 15 minutes

Caramelized Sugar Popcorn

10 cups of light popped corn unsalted
¼ teaspoon salt
½ cup of Splenda
2 teaspoons of light butter

Sprinkle salt over popcorn in large bowl and set aside. Place splenda in pan, heat over medium heat, shaking pan occasionally (DO NOT STIR) until splenda starts to melt. Reduce heat to low add butter stirring constantly until splenda is completely melted and golden. Add popcorn stirring to coat quickly transfer to large bowl cool.

Cranberry Spread

½ cup fat free sour cream
1–8 ounce package fat free cream cheese softened
¼ teaspoon ground cinnamon
2 tablespoons honey
1 can (16 ounces) whole berry cranberry sauce
1/3 cup silvered almond toasted

In a small mixing bowl, beat the cream cheese, sour cream, honey and cinnamon until smooth, spread onto a serving dish or plate. In a bowl stir cranberry sauce until it reach-spreading consistency. Spread over cream cheese mixture. Sprinkle with almonds cover and Refrigerate for 2–3 hours. Serve with crackers.
12–14 servings.

Cheese Sticks

1–3 ounce package fat free cream cheese softened
¾ cup carrots finely shredded
1 cup of 2% milk cheddar cheese finely shredded
½ cups pecans, finely chopped
24 thin pretzel sticks

Combine fat free cream cheese, carrots and cheese. Cover and chill for one hour. Shape into 1-inch balls and roll in pecans, chill. Before serving push one pretzel stick into each cheese ball.
Makes 24 servings

Dried Apple Slices

Granny Smith or cooking Apples peeled and thinly sliced
1-teaspoon ground cinnamon
¼ teaspoon ground cloves
¼ teaspoon ground allspices
½ teaspoon ground nutmeg
1 teaspoon Splenda

Mix spices and splenda in a Ziploc bag, add apple slices and toss gently to coat. Place apple slices on a cookie sheet covered with parchment paper. Dry apples in oven at 250 degrees for 1 to 1 ½ hours. Remove

from oven and cool. Apples will become crisper as they cool. Store in an airtight container
Makes 6 servings.

Cheese Deviled Eggs

6 Hard boiled eggs finely chopped
3 Bacon strips cooked and crumbled
¼ Cup of light mayonnaise
1 teaspoon minced onion
½ teaspoon salt, optional
½ teaspoon pepper, optional
¼ teaspoon prepared mustard
1 cup of 2% milk shredded cheddar cheese

In a bowl, combine the first seven ingredients until creamy. Shape into 1-inch balls. Roll in cheese. Cover and refrigerate until serving.
Makes about 2 dozen.

Glazed Mixed Nuts

½ cup brown splenda
½ teaspoon salt
1/8 teaspoon ground nutmeg
¼ teaspoon ground allspice
½ teaspoon ground cinnamon
4½ teaspoons water
2 cups mixed nuts

In a microwave safe bowl combine the first six ingredients. Stir in the water. Microwave uncovered on high for 1 minute. Stir, add nuts and stir until well coated. Cook uncovered on high for 4–5 minutes or until

syrup begins to harden, stirring after each minute immediately pour onto a greased foil lined baking sheet and separate nuts. Cool completely. Store in an airtight container.
Makes 2 ½ cups

Sweet Georgia Peanuts

1 cup Splenda
½ cup water
2 cups raw shelled peanuts, skin on
¼ teaspoon lite salt

Preheat oven to 300 degrees. Dissolve sugar and salt in water in saucepan over medium heat. Add peanuts. Continue to cook stirring frequently, until peanuts are completely sugared coated and no syrup is left. Pour onto ungreased cookie sheet, spreading so that peanut are separated as much as possible. Bake for approximately 30 minutes stirring at 5 minutes intervals. Let cool and serve

Hot Vidalia Onion Dip

Vidalia Onions are a Georgia favorite.

2 (8oz.) packages of lite cream cheese
3 cups chopped Vidalia onion
2 cups Parmesan cheese
½ cup light mayonnaise
Assorted crackers

Mix all ingredients well except crackers. Bake in a large baking dish at 425 degrees for 15 to 20 minutes. Serve with crackers

Vidalia Onion Dip

2 cups light mayonnaise
2 cups light grated Swiss cheese
2 cups chopped Vidalia onion
Crackers and chips

Mix and bake in a glass dish at 350 degrees for 25 minutes. Serve with crackers and chips.

Julie's Ranch Dip

Julie is my daughter's friend and she gave us this marvelous recipe.

1 package of Ranch dip mix
1–16 oz carton of light sour cream
1 cup of 2% milk sharp cheese
¼ cup of bacon bits

Mix first three ingredients and chill. Right before serving sprinkle bacon bits on top and serve with chips and crackers.

Cheese Nibblers

1 cup (4 oz.) finely shredded 2% milk cheddar cheese
1 cup crushed baked potato chips
½ cup all purpose flour
¼ cup lite butter softened
1 teaspoon ground mustard

In a bowl combine all ingredients. Shape dough into ¾ inch balls. Place on ungreased baking sheets and flatted slightly. Bake at 375 degrees for

5–8 minutes or until golden brown. Remove to a wire rack. Serve warm.
Yield: about 3 dozen

Ham 'n' Biscuits

2 cups all-purpose flour
1-tablespoon baking powder
½ teaspoon baking soda
1/8 teaspoon salt
1/3 cup cold light butter
1 cup reduced fat buttermilk
2 tablespoons light butter melted
1 (8oz.) package cooked country ham or regular ham slices
Mustard spread

Combine first 4 ingredients; cut in cold light butter with a pastry blender until mixture resembles coarse meal. Add buttermilk stirring until dry ingredients are moistened. Turn dough out onto a floured surface, and knead 4 or 5 times. Roll dough to ½ inch thickness; cut with a 1 ½ inch cutter. Place biscuits on an ungreased baking sheet; bake at 450 degrees for 10 to 12 minutes or until golden. Brush with melted butter. Serve with ham and mustard spread. Yield 2 dozen

Soups

Vegetable Soup

This is very good with cornbread.

4 cans diced tomatoes (14 ½ oz. Cans)
1 pound of ground beef
½ cup chopped onion
1 cup of cut up okra
2 cups of cut up potatoes
1 cup of lima beans
1 cup of corn

In a medium skillet brown ground beef and drain off fat. Mix ground beef and remaining ingredients. Cook slowly for 1 ½ hours.

Brunswick Stew

This was my late husband's recipe. I always enjoyed it when he cooked and gave me a night off in the kitchen.

1 whole chicken approximately 4 pounds
1 pound of lean ground beef
1 pound of hot sausage
3 cans of whole tomatoes
2 cans of cream style corn
1 can of whole kernel corn
1 small can tomato sauce

2 cups of Ketchup
18 teaspoons of Worcestershire sauce
¼ cup of A-1 sauce
½ cup fat free chicken broth
salt and pepper to taste

Cook chicken and shred into small pieces. Mix all ingredients together. Do not brown beef or sausage. Cook over medium to low heat stirring occasionally at beginning to allow beef and sausage to break up. Cook for 1 ½ to 2 hours

Slow Cooker Beef Stew

1 Beef Bouillon Cube
1 ½ pounds potatoes, peeled and cubed
3 medium carrots cut into 1 inch slices
1 medium onion chopped coarsely
3 tablespoons all purpose flour
1 ½ pounds beef stew meat cut into 1 inch cubes
3 tablespoons canola oil
1 can diced tomatoes undrained
2 cups of fat free beef broth
1 teaspoon ground mustard
½ teaspoon salt
½ teaspoon pepper
½ teaspoon dried thyme

Layer the potatoes, onions, and carrots, in a 5 quart slow cooker. Place flour in a large resealable plastic bag add stew meat, seal and toss to coat evenly. In a large skillet brown meat in oil in batches. Combine the tomatoes, broth, mustard, salt, pepper, and thyme. Cover and cook on high for 1–1 ½ hours reduce heat to low cook 7–8 hours longer or until the meat and vegetables are tender.
8 servings

Vegetable Ham Soup

My daughter says to get the ham bone from Honey Baked Ham. It makes this soup taste even better.

5 cups of water
2 cans (14 ½ ounces) diced tomatoes undrained
2 large carrots cut into 1 inch pieces
¾ cup chopped onion
½ cup chopped green pepper
1 tablespoon splenda
2 teaspoons dried basil
2 bay leaves
¼ cup cornstarch
¼ cup cold water
1 ham bone

In a crock pot combine the ingredients and cook on low for 1–1/4 hours or until vegetables or tender stirring occasionally. Combine cornstarch and cold water until smooth, stir into soup. Cook and stir until thickened. 11 servings

Turkey Vegetable Soup

8 cups fat free chicken broth
2 chicken bouillon cubes
½ to ¾ teaspoon pepper
2 cups sliced carrots
2 cups corn
¾ cups chopped onion
4 cups diced cooked turkey

In a crock pot combine the ingredients cook on low for 4 hours or high for 3 hours.

Onion Soup

2 cups thinly sliced sweet onions
6 tablespoons of light butter
1 can fat free chicken broth
2 teaspoons chicken bouillon granules
¼ teaspoon pepper
3 tablespoons all purpose flour
1 ½ cups 2% milk
¼ cup 2% milk cheddar cheese
minced fresh parsley

In a large skillet cook onions in 3 tablespoons light butter over medium low heat until tender add the broth add bouillon granules and pepper. Bring to a boil. Remove from the heat. In a large sauce pan melt the remaining butter. Stir in flour until smooth. Gradually add milk. Bring to a boil. Cook and stir for 1–2 minutes or until thickened. Reduce heat add cheese and onion mixture cook and stir until heated through and cheese is melted. Garnish with cheddar cheese and parsley

Charaman's Chili

This is my daughter's Charaman recipe for chili. I didn't know what a good cook she was until I tasted this wonderful chili.

1 pound of lean ground beef
½ small onion chopped
1 can of chili magic beans
4 cans of chili style tomatoes
1 small can of tomato sauce
1 envelope of chili seasoning

Brown ground beef and onion. Drain the meat. In a dutch oven combine the ground beef, beans, tomatoes, tomato sauce and chili seasoning. Bring to a boil reduce heat and simmer 10 minutes.

Vegetarian Soup

My daughter's friend Jackie is a vegetarian so we put in this recipe just for her.

1 cup chopped onion
2 garlic cloves minced
1 can (14 oz.) Healthy Choice Vegetable Broth
2 cans (15oz.) black beans, rinsed and drained
1 cup diced peeled potatoes
½ teaspoon dried thyme
½ teaspoon ground cumin
1 can (14 ½ oz.) diced tomatoes undrained
¼ to ½ teaspoon hot pepper sauce
2 green onions sliced.

In a saucepan bring the onion, garlic and ¼ cup broth to a boil. Reduce heat cover and simmer for 6–8 minutes or until onion is tender. Stir in the beans, potatoes, thyme, cumin and remaining broth. Return to a boil. Reduce heat cover and simmer for 20–25 minutes or until potatoes are tender. Stir in tomatoes and hot pepper sauce heat through. Sprinkle with green onion.
6 servings

Tomato Soup

2 cans (10 ¾ oz each) condensed tomatoes soup undiluted
2 2/3 cups skim milk
2 teaspoons chili powder

In a saucepan combine all the ingredients heat through and garnish with 2% milk sharp cheese.
4–5 servings

Chicken Soup

½ cup chopped onion
½ cup chopped carrot
1 tablespoon light butter
1 can (14 ½ oz.) fat free chicken broth
2/3 cup cubed cooked chicken
½ cup cauliflower
½ cup canned kidney beans rinsed and drained
¼ cup uncooked elbow macaroni
1/8 teaspoon pepper

In a saucepan sauté onion and carrot in butter for 4 minutes. Stir in the broth, chicken, beans, macaroni and cauliflower. Bring to a boil and reduce heat cover and simmer for 15–20 minutes or until macaroni and vegetables are tender
Servings 6

Mushroom Soup

This soup is cooked in the microwave so it is easy to fix.

¼ cup of light butter
½ pound sliced mushrooms
1 medium onion chopped
1 cup of fresh parsley
1 tablespoon all purpose flour
1 (14 oz.) can of fat free beef broth

In a baking dish heat the butter for 30 seconds in the microwave to melt. Add the mushrooms, onion and parsley and microwave for 5 minutes stirring once or twice. Stir in the flour and ½ cup of the beef broth. Cook uncovered for 1 to 2 minutes or until bubbly.
Servings 4

Navy Bean Soup

This soup takes a while to make but it is well worth it.

1 pound dried navy beans
1 can fat free chicken broth
2 tablespoon minced fresh parsley
2 bay leaves
¼ teaspoon pepper
1 medium onion chopped
1 medium carrot chopped
6 turkey bacon strips cooked and crumbled

Place beans in a dutch oven. Add water to cover by 2 inches bring to a boil for 2 minutes. Remove from heat cover and let stand for 1 hour. Drain and rinse beans discarding liquid. In a large saucepan combine the broth, beans, parsley, bay leaves and pepper. Bring to a boil. Reduce heat cover and simmer for 1 hour. Add the onion and carrots cover and simmer for 20–25 minutes or until vegetable and beans are tender stir in bacon. Discard the bay leaves before serving.
8–10 servings

Salads

Cherry Waldorf Salad

2 large apples (chopped)
1 tablespoon lemon juice
1 cup fresh or frozen pitted tart cherries halved
½ cup dried cranberries
½ cup walnuts
¼ cup light mayonnaise
¼ cup light sour cream
2 tablespoon honey
1/8 teaspoon salt

In a large salad bowl toss apples with lemon juice. Add cherries cranberries and walnuts. In a small bowl, whisk the mayonnaise, sour cream, honey and salt until well blended. Pour over salad and toss to coat cover and refrigerate for 1 hour before serving.
6–8 servings

Avocado Mandarin Salad

1 can (11 oz.) mandarin oranges drained
1/3 cup coarsely chopped pecans, toasted
1/8 teaspoon pepper
4 cups torn salad greens
1 medium ripe avocado peeled and sliced
¼ cup prepared Italian salad dressing

In a bowl combine the oranges pecans and pepper refrigerate for 30 minutes. Just before serving place the greens in a salad bowl, top with orange mixture and avocadoes slices, drizzle with dressing
8 servings

Cheddar Broccoli Salad

6 cups of Broccoli florets
1 ½ cups of 2% milk Sharp Cheddar cheese shredded
1/3 cup chopped onion
1 ½ cups light mayonnaise
¾ cup splenda
3 tablespoons cider vinegar
12 turkey bacon strips cooked and crumbled

In a large bowl combine the broccoli cheese and onion combine the mayonnaise splenda and vinegar. Pour over broccoli mixture and toss to coat. Refrigerate for at least 4 hours right before serving stir in the bacon.
Servings 8

Apple Lettuce Salad

½ cup unsweetened apple juice
2 tablespoon lemon juice
2 tablespoon cider vinegar
2 tablespoon canola oil
4 ½ teaspoons brown splenda
1 teaspoons pepper
1/8 teaspoon salt
1/8 teaspoon ground cinnamon
Dash ground nutmeg
1 medium green apple chopped

1 medium red apple chopped
6 cups torn green leaf lettuce
6 cups torn red leaf lettuce

In a large salad bowl, whisk the first 10 ingredients until blended add apples toss to coat, place, lettuce over apple mixture (do not toss). Refrigerate. Toss just before serving.
12 servings

Salad and Vinaigrette Dressing

¾ cup olive oil
¼ cup white wine vinegar
1 teaspoon salt
1 teaspoon dry mustard
½ teaspoon splenda
½ teaspoon garlic powder
3 to 4 drops hot pepper sauce
salad greens
bell peppers, mushrooms, tomatoes and other vegetables of your choice

In a jar with a tight fitting lid combine the first seven ingredients and shake well. Toss salad greens and vegetables in a large bowl and pour dressing over greens and serve.
1 cup dressing.

Garden Chicken Salad

¾ cup light mayonnaise
3 tablespoon skim milk
2 tablespoon green onion
1 teaspoon grated lemon peel

2 teaspoons lemon juice
1 teaspoon splenda
¼ teaspoon pepper
6 cups cut up fresh vegetables
Lettuce leaves to line platter
1 pound boneless skinless chicken breast grilled and sliced

Combine first seven ingredients in a small bowl for the dressing. In a large bowl toss vegetables with half of dressing. Arrange a lettuce lined platter and top with vegetables. Top with chicken serve with dressing.
Serves 4

Fruited Chicken Salad

1 can (20 oz.) pineapple chunks in juice undrained
½ cup miracle whip free non fat dressing
1 tablespoon Dijon mustard
1 teaspoon curry powder
½ teaspoon salt
4 cups chopped chicken
½ cup golden raisins
¼ cup walnuts
½ cup chopped celery

Drain pineapple reserving 3 tablespoons liquid. Mix reserved 3 tablespoon liquid, miracle whip, mustard, curry and salt in large bowl. Add pineapple and remaining ingredients mix lightly. Refrigerate. Spoon chicken mixture over lettuce lined platter.
Makes 4 to 6 servings

Chicken Rice Waldorf Salad

1 ½ cups instant brown rice
1 cup light mayonnaise
1 large red apple diced
1 tablespoon lemon juice
2 cups diced cooked chicken
1 cup seedless green grapes

Prepare rice as directed on package. Mix in mayonnaise. Mix apple with lemon juice. Stir into rice mixture with remaining ingredients chill.
6 servings

Turkey Apple Salad

1 can (5 oz.) white or white and dark turkey drained
¾ cup chopped apple
2 tablespoons raisins
1/3 cup prepared Italian dressing
1 tablespoon brown splenda

In a medium bowl, gently stir together chunk turkey, apple and raisins. In another bowl, stir together dressing and brown splenda pour over turkey mixture. Toss gently to coat. Serve on lettuce.
Makes 2–½ cup servings

Chicken Salad

2 cups cubed cooked chicken
1 cup light mayonnaise
½ to 1 teaspoon curry powder
1 can (20 oz.) chunk pineapple drained

2 large firm bananas sliced
1 can (11 oz.) mandarin oranges, drained
½ cup flake coconut
salad greens optional
¾ cup salted peanuts

Place chicken in a large bowl. Combine mayonnaise and curry powder. Add to chicken and mix well. Cover and chill for at least 30 minutes. Before serving add the pineapple, bananas, oranges and coconut toss gently. Serve on salad greens if desired. Sprinkle with nuts.
4–6 servings

Chinese Chicken Salad

3 cups torn lettuce
1 ½ cup chopped cooked chicken
1 (8 oz) can sliced water chestnuts drained
½ cup julienne carrots
¼ cup chopped red cabbage
¼ cup diagonally sliced green onions
1 (5 oz) can chow mein noodles

Dressing
3½ tablespoons light soy sauce
2 tablespoons each of canola oil and rice vinegar
1 teaspoon splenda
½ teaspoon each of garlic powder, pepper and sesame oil

In a large bowl whisk dressing ingredients. Add lettuce, chicken and vegetables toss with dressing top with chow mein noodles.
Servings 4–6

Holiday Sugar Free Gelatin Salad

This is a holiday favorite.

1 (4 serving) package sugar free lime gelatin
3 cups of boiling water
1 (8oz.) package fat free cream cheese
1 cup (8oz. can) crushed pineapple packed in its own juice drained
2 teaspoons splenda
½ teaspoon vanilla extract
¼ cup (1 oz.) chopped pecans
1 (4 serving) package sugar free strawberry gelatin

In a medium bowl combine dry lime gelatin and 1 ½ cups boiling water. Mix well to dissolve gelatin. Pour mixture into an 8 by 8 inch dish. Refrigerate until set, about 2 hours. In a medium bowl stir cream cheese with a spoon until soft. Add drained pineapple, splenda, vanilla extract and pecans to the cream cheese. Mix well to combine. Spread mixture over set gelatin. Meanwhile in a medium bowl combine dry strawberry gelatin and remaining 1 ½ cups boiling water mix well to dissolve gelatin. Refrigerate gelatin mixture for about 15 minutes. Pour cooled strawberry gelatin evenly over cream cheese layer. Refrigerate for at least 2 hours when serving cut into 8 pieces.

Strawberry Nut Salad

3 packages (3 oz each) sugar free strawberry flavored gelatin
1 cup water
2 packages frozen strawberries drained
1 large can crushed pineapple drained
2 teaspoons lemon juice
3 bananas chopped
1 cup nuts chopped
1 pint light sour cream

Dissolve gelatin in boiling water, add strawberry, pineapple, lemon juice, bananas and nuts. Put half of the mixture (2–2 ½ cups) in an 8x12x12 pan chill to set. Pour sour cream over mixture. Then carefully spoon rest of strawberry mixture over sour cream. Refrigerate until firm
Servings 12

Chicken Salad on Cantaloupe Rings

2½ cups cubed cooked chicken
1 cup thinly sliced celery
1 cup of green grapes halved
2 tablespoons mince fresh parsley
½ cup light mayonnaise
1 tablespoon lemon juice
1 tablespoon cider vinegar
1 ½ teaspoon prepared mustard
½ teaspoon salt
½ teaspoon splenda
1/8 teaspoon pepper
4 cantaloupe rings
toasted sliced almonds

In a large bowl combine chicken, celery, grapes, and parsley. Combine the next seven ingredients mix well. Pour over chicken mixture and toss. Chill for at least 1 hour. To serve place 1 cup of chicken salad on each cantaloupe ring. Sprinkle with almonds.
4 servings

Caesar Salad

3 tablespoons olive oil
4 ½ teaspoon lemon juice

1 teaspoon prepared mustard
1 teaspoon garlic powder
6 cups torn romaine lettuce
2/3 cup Caesar salad croutons
½ cup 2% milk Cheddar Cheese shredded
Coarsely ground pepper to taste

In a jar with tight fitting lid combine the oil, lemon juice, mustard and garlic and shake well. In a salad bowl combine the romaine lettuce, croutons, cheese and pepper. Drizzle with dressing and toss to coat.
4 servings

Raspberry Salad

10 cups torn mixed greens
3 cups fresh or frozen unsweetened raspberries
2 tablespoons olive oil
3 tablespoons cider vinegar
4 teaspoons splenda
1/8 teaspoon salt
dash pepper

In a large salad bowl, gently combine the salad greens and 2 ¾ cup raspberries. Mash the remaining berries strain reserving juice and discarding seeds. In a bowl, whisk the raspberry juice, oil, vinegar, splenda, salt and pepper. Drizzle over salad gently toss to coat.
12 servings

Cashew Tossed Salad

1/3 cup white vinegar
¾ cup splenda

3 teaspoons prepared mustard
1 tablespoon grated onion
Dash salt
1 cup olive oil
1 medium bunch romaine lettuce torn
1 cup salted cashew halves
4 ounces 2% milk sharp cheddar cheese shredded

In a blender combine the vinegar, splenda, mustard, onion and salt cover and process until well blended. While processing gradually add oil in a steady stream. In a salad bowl combine the romaine lettuce, cashews and shredded cheese. Serve with dressing.
8–10 servings

Tuna Salad

½ cup drained water packed tuna
1 cup low fat cottage cheese
1 hard boiled egg, peeled and chopped
1 tablespoon parsley
1 teaspoon lemon pepper seasoning
¼ teaspoon seasoned salt
¼ cup diet mayonnaise

In a mixing bowl combine all ingredients chill.
4 servings

Stuffed Apple Ring Salad

2 to 3 Red Delicious apples
Pineapple juice or lemon juice
1–8 oz package light cream cheese softened

2 to 3 tablespoon splenda
1/3 cup seedless green grapes
¼ cup chopped pecans
Lettuce leaves

Core unpeeled apples and cut into ¾ inch thick rings. Dip in pineapple juice or lemon juice to prevent browning. Set aside. Place cream cheese in a small mixing bowl beat at medium speed with an electric mixer until smooth. Add splenda beat at medium speed until light and fluffy. Stir in grapes and pecans. Arrange apples rings on lettuce leaves. Pipe or dollop cream cheese mixture into center of each apple ring.
5 servings.

Julie's Fruit Salad

Here is another wonderful recipe from my daughter's friend Julie.

1 (8oz) package of light cream cheese
1 (8oz) carton of light sour cream
1 cup splenda
1 teaspoon vanilla
Assorted fruit

Mix first four ingredients. Mix in fruit. Chill until ready to serve.

Vegetables

Creamed Cabbage

1 turkey bacon strip diced
2 tablespoons chopped onion
1 tablespoon cider vinegar
1 tablespoon water
1 ¼ teaspoon splenda
¼ teaspoon salt
¼ teaspoon pepper
2 cups shredded cabbage
1 small tart apple peeled and chopped
¼ cup lite sour cream

In a skillet cook bacon over medium heat until crisp. Remove to paper towel. In the drippings sauté onion until tender. Add the vinegar, water, splenda, salt and pepper. Cook until bubbly. Stir in cabbage and apple toss to coat. Cover and cook for 5–6 minutes or until cabbage is tender. Stir in sour cream and heat through but do not boil. Sprinkle with bacon.

Fried Green Tomatoes

There is nothing as good as Fried Green Tomatoes.

3 or 4 large firm green tomatoes
½ cup cornmeal
½ teaspoon lite salt
¼ teaspoon black pepper

1 egg
1 tablespoon water
1 tablespoon oil

Brush oil on a 15x10 inch jellyroll pan. Combine cornmeal, salt and pepper in bowl and set aside. Beat egg and water together. Set aside. Dip tomato slices in egg mixture. Dredge in cornmeal mixture to coat. Place tomatoes slices in a single layer. Coat tomatoes with cooking spray and bake at 450 degrees for 8 minutes. Turn over and spray with cooking spray again, bake an additional 7 to 8 minutes after last baking, broil 4 inches from heat 4 to 5 minutes or until browned turn over occasionally 6 servings

Oven Fried Okra

My family has always loved fried okra and they love the oven fried even better.

1 pound fresh okra
1 large egg
¼ cup light buttermilk
2/3 cup cornmeal
1/3 cup all purpose flour
1 teaspoon baking powder
½ teaspoon salt
1 tablespoon vegetable oil
butter flavored cooking spray

Wash okra and drain. Remove tips and stem ends. Cut okra crosswise into ½ inch slices. Combine egg and buttermilk, stir in okra and let stand 10 minutes. Combine cornmeal and next 3 ingredients in a zip lock plastic bag or in a batter bowl. Drain okra, small portions at a time using a slotted spoon, place okra in bag with cornmeal mixture shaking

gently to coat. Brush olive oil on a 15x10x1 inch jellyroll pan. Add okra in a single layer. Coat okra with cooking spray and bake at 450 degrees for 8 minutes, Stir well and spray with cooking spray again bake an additional 7 to 8 minutes. After last baking broil 4 inches from heat 4 to 5 minutes or until browned, stirring occasionally
8 servings

Oven French Fries

½ cup grated Parmesan cheese
2 teaspoons dried oregano
2 (8oz.) baking potatoes unpeeled
1 egg white beaten
Vegetable cooking spray

Combine Parmesan cheese and oregano set aside. Cut each potato lengthwise into 8 wedges, dip into egg white and dredge in Parmesan cheese mixture. Place fries on a baking sheet coated with vegetable cooking spray. Bake at 425 degrees for 25 minutes.
4 servings

Oven Fried Zucchini Spears

3 tablespoons herb seasoned bread crumbs
1 tablespoon grated Parmesan cheese
1/8 teaspoon paprika
1/8 teaspoon pepper
2 medium zucchini (about 12 oz)
2 teaspoons olive oil
2 tablespoons water
Vegetable cooking spray

Combine bread crumbs, Parmesan cheese, paprika and pepper in a shallow dish, set aside. Cut each zucchini lengthwise into 4 pieces, cut each piece in half crosswise. Place zucchini in a zip lock plastic bag. Add oil and water shake. Dredge zucchini in breadcrumb mixture and place on a baking sheet coated with cooking spray.
Bake at 475 degrees for 10 minutes or until brown and tender.
4 servings

Carrots and Pineapple

2 cups baby carrots
1 can (20oz) Pineapple chunks packed in its own juice
4 teaspoons cornstarch
½ teaspoon cinnamon
½ cup brown splenda
1 tablespoon of light butter

In a saucepan bring 1 inch of water to a boil, place carrots in a steamer basket over water. Cover and steam for 10 minutes or until crisp tender. Drain pineapple reserving juice set pineapple aside. In a sauce pan combine cornstarch and cinnamon add the brown splenda butter and reserved juice. Bring to a boil. Cook and stir for 2 minutes or until thickened. Stir in the carrots and pineapple and heat through.
4 servings

Squash Casserole

1 large onion chopped
4 tablespoon of light butter
3 cups cooked squash drained with all water squeezed out
1 cup crushed Whole Wheat Ritz Crackers plus additional for topping
½ cup light sour cream

salt and pepper to taste
1 cup 2% milk grated cheddar cheese

Preheat oven 350 degrees. Sauté onion in butter for 5 minutes. Remove from pan mix all ingredients together. Pour into buttered spray casserole dish and top with cracker crumbs. Bake for 25 to 30 minutes.

Broccoli Casserole

1–10 oz package frozen chopped broccoli
1 small onion chopped
4 tablespoon light butter
½ cup grated 2% milk cheddar cheese
½ cup crushed whole wheat Ritz crackers
½ cup Healthy Request Cream of Mushroom soup
¼ cup light mayonnaise
salt and pepper to taste
1–8 oz. Can sliced water chestnut drained

Preheat oven to 350 degrees. Steam broccoli until limp, about 10 minutes remove from heat drain. Sauté onion in butter and add to broccoli. Add all remaining ingredients mix well. Pour mixture into a casserole dish add topping ½ cup crushed Ritz crackers. Bake for 20 to 25 minutes.

Vegetable Casserole

This is my son's favorite casserole.

1–15 oz can veg all drained
1–8 oz can sliced water chestnuts drained
1–cup grated 2 % milk sharp cheese
1 cup mushrooms

1 small onion chopped
20 whole wheat Ritz crackers crushed
½ cup light mayonnaise
2 tablespoon light butter

In a large bowl mix the veg all, water chestnuts, cheese, mushrooms, mayonnaise and onion transfer to a casserole dish sprayed with butter flavor spray. Baked at 350 degrees for 30 minutes. Combine cracker crumbs and butter sprinkle on top of casserole and return to the oven to brown.

Broccoli Mustard Sauce

4 cups fresh or frozen broccoli florets
½ cup water
½ teaspoon salt divided
1 tablespoon of light butter
1 tablespoon all purpose flour
½ cup plus 2 tablespoon of skim evaporated milk
1 ½ teaspoon prepared mustard
¼ teaspoon dill weed

In a large saucepan bring the broccoli water and ¼ teaspoon salt to a boil. Reduce heat cover and simmer for 5–8 minutes or until broccoli is crisp tender. In a small sauce pan melt butter. Stir in flour until smooth. Gradually stir in milk until thickened. Stir in the mustard, dill and remaining salt. Drain broccoli drizzle with the mustard sauce
4 servings

Colorful Veggie Bake

2 packages (16oz.) frozen California Blend vegetables
10 ounce process cheese cubed

6 tablespoons light butter
½ cup whole wheat Ritz Crackers

Prepare vegetables according to package directions and drain. Place half in an ungreased 11in x 7in x 2in baking dish. In a small saucepan, combine cheese and 4 tablespoons butter cook and stir over low heat until melted pour half over vegetables. Repeat layers. Melt the remaining butter, toss with crackers crumbs, sprinkle over the top. Bake uncovered at 325 degrees for 20–25 minutes or until golden brown.
8–10 servings

Broccoli Casserole

2 pounds fresh broccoli cut into florets
1 can (10 ¾ oz) Healthy Choice Cream of Mushrooms soup
½ cup light mayonnaise
½ cup 2% milk shredded cheddar cheese
1 tablespoon lemon juice
1 cup crushed cheese flavored snack crackers

Place one inch of water and broccoli in a saucepan bring to a boil. Reduce heat cover and simmer for 5–8 minutes or just until crisp and tender. Drain and place in a greased 2 quart baking dish. In a bowl combine the soup, mayonnaise, cheese and lemon juice. Pour over broccoli. Sprinkle with crushed crackers. Bake uncovered at 350 degrees for 25–30 minutes or until heated through.
6–8 Servings

Roasted Brussels Sprouts with Bacon

4 packages (10 oz each) fresh or frozen Brussels Sprouts trimmed and halved lengthwise about 8 cups

4 large shallots sliced 1 cup
6 slices bacon cut in ½ pieces
2 teaspoons light butter melted
1 teaspoons salt
½ teaspoons dried thyme
¼ teaspoons pepper

Preheat oven to 425 degrees. In large bowl combine Brussels sprouts, shallots, bacon, butter, salt, thyme and pepper. Toss to coat. Spread mixture in large ungreased pan. Roast until lightly browned and tender 20–25 minutes.
8 servings

Cabbage Casserole

1 head cabbage chopped
8 slices bacon
1 medium onion chopped
1 medium green bell pepper chopped
1 (10 ¾ oz) can Healthy Choice Cream of Mushroom Soup
¾ cup 2% milk grated cheddar cheese
½ cup skim milk
1 teaspoon salt
3 slices whole wheat bread toasted and crumble
1 stick lite butter melted

Cook the cabbage for 8 minutes in salted water. Drain. Preheat the oven to 350 degrees. Fry the bacon in a saucepan until crisp. In the same saucepan sauté the onion and pepper until the onion and pepper is soft. In a large bowl combine the cabbage, bacon, soup, cheese, milk and salt. Pour the mixture in a casserole dish. Toss the toasted bread in the melted butter and spread it on top of the casserole. Bake for 35 minutes.
6–8 servings

Asparagus Casserole

2 tablespoons light butter
2 tablespoons all purpose flour
2 cup skim milk
2 (15oz) cans asparagus spears drained
1 cup 2% Milk Cheddar Cheese
4 hard boiled eggs sliced
salt and pepper
1 cup whole wheat Ritz Cracker crumbs

To make the sauce, heat the butter stir in the flour mixing well, then add the milk all at once. Cook over medium heat stirring constantly until thick and creamy, set aside, arrange half of the asparagus in the bottom of a buttered 2 quart casserole. Top with half of the cheddar and half of the egg slices. Sprinkle with salt and pepper to taste. Pour half of the sauce on top. Repeat the layers beginning with the remaining asparagus top with the cracker crumbs bake for 25 to 30 minutes.

Green Bean Casserole

2 cups baked potato chips
¾ cup skin milk
1/8 teaspoon ground black pepper
1–10 ¾ oz. Can Healthy Choice Cream of Mushroom soup
2 (9oz) packages of frozen French cut green beans thawed
1 1/3 cup original French fried onions

In a 9 inch square oven proof dish layer one package of green beans. Then layer 2/3 cup French fried onion then 1 cup crumbled potatoes chips. Then another package of green beans. Another 2/3 cup of French fried onion, then 1 cup crumbled potatoes chips. In a medium bowl mix cream of mushroom soup with milk and pepper. Pour soup mixture over casserole layers. Bake at 350 degrees for 45 minutes until bubbly. Remove from oven top with 1 cup crumbled potatoes chips. Serve hot.

Mushroom Oven Rice

1 cup uncooked long grain brown rice
¼ cup light butter
½ cup finely chopped celery
½ cup finely chopped onion
1 cup sliced fresh mushrooms
1 can (14–12 oz) Healthy Choice Chicken Broth
½ cup water
1 to 2 tablespoon light soy sauce
1 tablespoon dried parsley flakes

In a skillet sauté the rice in butter for 2 minutes. Add celery and onion, cook and stir for 2 minutes or until celery is tender, add mushrooms. Transfer to a greased 1 ½ quart baking dish. Stir in the broth, water, soy sauce and parsley cover and bake at 350 degrees for 45–50 minutes or until liquid is absorbed and rice is tender
6 servings

Carrot Broccoli Casserole

1 package (16 oz) baby carrots
1 ½ pound of fresh broccoli chopped or 2 packages (10 oz each) frozen chopped broccoli thawed
8 oz 2% milk sharp cheddar cheese cut in small cubes
¾ cups light butter
1 ¾ cup crushed wheat Ritz crackers (about 40 crackers)

Place one inch of water in a saucepan add carrots. Bring to a boil. Reduce heat cover and simmer for 5–8 minutes or until crisp. Add broccoli cover

and simmer 6–8 minutes longer or until vegetables are tender. Drain and set aside. In a small saucepan cook and stir the cheese and ¼ cup butter until smooth. Stir in the broccoli and carrots until combined melt the remaining butter toss with cracker crumbs. Sprinkle a third of the mixture in a greased 2 ½ quart baking dish top with half of the vegetable mixture. Repeat layers sprinkle with the remaining crumb mixture. Bake uncovered at 350 degrees for 35–40 minutes or until heated through.
6–8 servings

Southern Style Black-eye Peas

1–16oz package frozen black-eye peas
1 quart of water
2 beef bouillon cubes
2 tablespoons butter
¼ teaspoon salt
¼ teaspoon pepper
½ teaspoon Texas Pete Hot Sauce

Put water in a stockpot bring to a boil. Add the peas and beef bouillon cubes, butter, salt, pepper and Texas Pete hot sauce. Reduce the heat. Cover and cook over low heat for 20 to 30 minutes or until the peas are done.
4–6 Servings

Turnip Greens

2 lbs fresh turnip greens
1 smoked ham bone
Salt to taste

Wash greens thoroughly cut meat into slices. Put greens and meat into a stockpot. Add water and cook until meat and greens are tender about 30 minutes. Add salt and pepper to taste.

Pinto Beans

1 lb pinto beans
2 beef bouillon cubes
1 teaspoon salt
dash black pepper
¼ teaspoon parsley
¼ teaspoon bay leaves
3 drops hot sauce
2 tablespoons olive oil

Wash beans and soak in 6 cups cold water over night. Drain and cover with 6 cups fresh cold water. Turn heat on medium. Add salt and pepper. Beef bouillon, parsley, bay leaves, hot sauce to beans. Cook 4 to 5 hours and add more water as needed.

Hoppin John

2 cups black eyed peas, cooked
2 cups cooked brown rice
1 small onion
1 small bell pepper chopped
Salt and pepper to taste

Heat the black-eyed peas and add the rice. Add remaining ingredients and cook an additional 10 to 15 minutes.

Corn Pudding

1 (12 oz.) can whole kernel corn
2 (17 oz.) cans cream style corn
5 eggs, lightly beaten
½ cup splenda
4 tablespoons cornstarch
1 ½ teaspoons seasoned salt
½ teaspoon dry mustard
1 teaspoon minced onion
½ cup skim milk
½ cup melted light butter

Combine corn and eggs. Mix together splenda, cornstarch, salt, mustard and onion. Add to corn mixture. Stir in milk and butter.
Pour into greased 3 quart casserole.
Bake at 400 degrees for 1 hour stirring once.
Yield: 6 servings

Vegetable Medley

1 package frozen mixed vegetables
1 cup 2% milk Cheddar Cheese
1 cup light mayonnaise
1 onion, chopped
1 stick light butter melted
1 cup reduced fat small cheese crackers

Cook frozen vegetables for 10 minutes and drain. Mix the next 3 ingredients together. Add to drained vegetables.

Mix cheese crackers with butter until coated. Top the casserole with cheese crackers. Bake at 350 degrees for 30 minutes, uncovered, in an 8x8 inch square baking dish.
Yield: 8 servings

Cheesy Pineapple Casserole

1 (20 oz.) can pineapple tidbits in natural juice, juice reserved
½ cup splenda
3 tablespoons flour
1 1/3 cups 2% finely shredded sharp cheddar cheese
1 ½ cups crushed reduced fat round crackers
½ stick light margarine, melted

Pour pineapple and reserved juice into bottom of greased 7x11 inch casserole dish. Mix splenda, flour and cheese together. Sprinkle on top of pineapple. Combine cracker crumbs and margarine. Sprinkle on top of cheese mixture. Bake at 350 degrees in a preheated over for 30 minutes.
Yield: 8–10 servings

Zucchini & Onion with Mozzarella

3 tablespoons light butter
3 cups sliced zucchini
1 cup sliced onion
½ teaspoon basil leaves
¼ teaspoon oregano leaves
Pinch of lite salt
½ teaspoon garlic
1 medium ripe tomato cut into wedges
1 cup light shredded mozzarella cheese

In a 10 inch skillet melt butter over medium heat. Add remaining ingredients except tomato and cheese. Continue cooking stirring occasionally, until zucchini is crisply tender (7 to 10 minutes) Add tomato wedges; sprinkle with cheese. Cover; let stand 2 minutes or until cheese is melted.

Glazed Baby Carrots

1 cup baby carrots
1 tablespoon light butter
2 teaspoons orange juice
1 teaspoon splenda
¼ teaspoon ground mustard
Pepper to taste

Place carrots in a saucepan; add 1 inch of water. Bring to a boil. Reduce heat. Cover and simmer for 5 minutes or until crisp-tender. Meanwhile, in a small saucepan, melt butter. Add orange juice, splenda, mustard and pepper, cook and stir until thickened. Drain carrots; drizzle with butter mixture.

Herbed Tomatoes

4 medium Tomatoes cut into thin slices
4 slices sweet Vidalia onion, separated into rings
8 teaspoons olive oil
1 ½ teaspoon lemon juice
¼ teaspoon minced garlic
1 teaspoon each minced fresh tarragon, basil and parsley
salt and pepper to taste

In a bowl combine the tomatoes and onion. In another bowl, combine the oil, lemon juice, garlic, herbs, salt and pepper. Pour over tomatoes and onion stir gently to coat.
Yield: 4 servings

Sweet Slaw

2 cups shredded cabbage
¼ cup finely chopped onion
2 tablespoons shredded carrot
2 tablespoons finely chopped green pepper

Dressing
¼ cup light mayonnaise
2 tablespoons unsweetened crushed pineapple drained
1 tablespoon unsweetened pineapple juice
1 tablespoon cider vinegar
2 teaspoon splenda
¼ teaspoon lite salt
1/8 teaspoon pepper

In a small bowl, combine the cabbage, onion, carrot, celery and green pepper. Combine the dressing ingredients; pour over cabbage mixture and toss to coat. Cover and refrigerate for at least 1 hour before serving.

Hot Hominy Casserole

2 (15 ½ oz) cans yellow or white hominy drained
1 (4 oz.) can green chilies
½ cup grated onion
8 oz. Low fat sour cream
6 strips turkey bacon crisply cooked and crumbled

salt and pepper
1 ½ cups grated 2% milk sharp cheddar cheese

Preheat the oven to 350 degrees. Lightly grease an 8 inch casserole dish. Combine the hominy chilies and onion. Stir in the sour cream, bacon, salt and pepper. Spoon into the prepared dish. Sprinkle the cheese evenly over the top. Cover with foil and bake for 20 minutes. Remove the foil and bake for an additional 10 minutes or until golden and bubbly.
8 to 10 servings

Macaroni and Cheese

My daughter has always loved Macaroni and Cheese. When she was trying to lose weight she stopped eating it but now she can eat it again the healthy way.

8oz. box of whole wheat elbow macaroni
1 cup skim milk
2 eggs
1 teaspoon salt
¼ teaspoon pepper
3 cups shredded 2% milk sharp cheese

Cook Macaroni according to package directions and drain.
In a bowl stir together milk and eggs, salt and pepper.
In a baking dish place a layer of macaroni then a layer of cheese. Dot with light butter continued with layers of macaroni and cheese until macaroni is gone. Pour egg and milk mixture over all and let settle through mixture. Top with cheese and bake at 350 degrees for 30 minutes until brown and bubbly.

Avanti's Grits

I never really liked grits until my daughter cooked grits like her friend Avanti did. These are the best grits I have ever had.

1 cup uncooked grits
1 stick light butter
1–8oz package lite cream cheese

Cook grits in 4 cups salted water, as the grits just begin to get thick add the stick of lite butter. Continue cooking grits. When the grits are almost thick enough to eat add the cream cheese and stir until dissolved.

Sweet Potatoes Surprise

3 medium sweet potatoes
1 cup pecans
1 cup coconut
1 cup raisins
1 cup splenda
2 tablespoons butter

Mix all ingredient except butter. Place in a oven proof pan dot with butter and cook at 350 degrees for 45 minutes. Stirring often.

Thanksgiving Dressing

2 ½ cups dry bread torn into small pieces
3 cups of corn bread crumbled
4 cups of fat free chicken broth
½ cup of light margarine
½ cup of onion

4 eggs
½ teaspoon pepper
½ teaspoon salt
2 tablespoons of sage
1 can of cream of chicken & mushroom soup

Combine all Ingredients and place in a oven proof pan. Bake at 350 degrees for 45 minutes.

Meats

Chicken

Roasted Chicken

1 Broiler chicken
½ teaspoon dried thyme
2 teaspoons salt divided
1 large onion, cut into eighths
4 fresh parsley springs

Sprinkle inside of chicken with thyme and 1 teaspoon salt stuff with onion and parsley sprig. Place in a greased dutch oven cover and bake at 375 degrees for 30 minutes.
4 servings

Marinated Baked Chicken

½ cup Italian light salad dressing
½ cup light soy sauce
6 bone in chicken breast halves
1/8 teaspoon onion salt
1/8 teaspoon garlic salt
Spiced apple rings optional

In a measuring cup combine salad dressing and soy sauce. Pour ¾ cup into a large resealable plastic bag. Add Chicken. Seal the bag and turn to coat.

Refrigerate for 4 hours or overnight turning several times. Refrigerate remaining marinade for basting. Drain Chicken discarding marinade. Place chicken skin side up on a rack in a roasting pan. Sprinkle with onion salt and garlic salt. Bake uncovered at 350 degree for 45–60 minutes or until juices run clear and meat thermometer reads 170 degrees brushing occasionally with reserved marinade. Garnish platter with apple rings.
6 servings

Parmesan Chicken

1 cup all purpose flour
2 teaspoon salt
2 teaspoon paprika
2 eggs
3 tablespoon skim milk
2/3 cup grated parmesan cheese
1/3 cup whole wheat dry bread crumbs
1 boiler fryer chicken 3 to 4 pounds cut up

In a bowl, combine the parmesan cheese and bread crumbs. Coat chicken pieces with flour mixture, dip in egg mixture then roll in crumb mixture. Place in a well-greased 15 inch x 10 inch x 1 inch baking pan. Bake at 400 degrees for 50–55 minutes or until chicken juices run clear.
4 servings

Chicken Tarragon

4 boneless skinless chicken breast halves
½ teaspoon paprika
1/3 cup light butter divided
2 medium zucchini julienne
4 small carrots jullined

4 large mushrooms sliced
2 tablespoons minced fresh tarragon or one teaspoon of dried tarragon.
1 tablespoon lemon juice
½ teaspoon salt
1/8 teaspoon pepper

Sprinkle chicken with paprika. In a large skillet brown chicken in a teaspoon of butter. Place the vegetables in a greased 9 x 9 inch baking dish. Top with chicken melt the remaining butter stir in the tarragon, lemon juice salt and pepper. Pour over chicken and vegetables. Cover and bake at 350 degrees for 30–35 minutes or until chicken juices run clear and vegetables are tender.
4 servings

Apricot Chicken

4 to 6 boneless skinless chicken breast
2 (12 oz.) jars apricot preserves low sugar or sugar free
1 envelope onion soup mix

Place chicken in slow cooker. Combine the preserves and soup mix. Spoon over chicken cover and cook for 4 to 6 hours or until chicken is tender.
4–6 servings

Chicken with Sour Cream Gravy

½ cup all purpose flour
2 teaspoons paprika
1 teaspoon each salt, pepper, garlic powder and cayenne pepper
2 teaspoons light butter
4 boneless chicken breast halves
1 can (10 ¾ oz) Health Choice Cream of Chicken Soup

¼ cup sliced green onions
1–8 oz. carton fat free sour cream

Mix flour and seasonings coat chicken. Melt light butter in skillet add chicken and cook until browned. Add soup and onion cover and cook over low heat 10 minutes or until done. Stir in sour cream.
4 servings

Apricot Honey Chicken Poupon

This is one of my daughter's favorite recipe for chicken.

1/3 Cup Grey Poupon Honey Mustard
3 tablespoon sugar free Apricot Preserves
1 teaspoon ground ginger
4 boneless skinless chicken breast halves

Blend mustard, apricot preserves and ginger. Brush some mustard mixture on chicken. Grill or broil chicken for 6 to 8 minutes on each side or until done, brushing with mustard mixture frequently.
Makes 4 servings

Baked Chicken Poupon

4 teaspoons Grey Poupon Dijon Mustard
2 teaspoons olive oil
1 teaspoon garlic powder
½ teaspoon Italian seasoning
1 pound boneless chicken breast

Mix Grey Poupon Dijon mustard, oil, garlic powder and Italian seasoning in a large bowl or plastic bag. Add chicken mixing to coat bake at 375 degrees for 20 minutes or until done.
4 servings

Walnut Chicken Skillet

2 teaspoon cornstarch divided
3 tablespoon light soy sauce divided
1 pound boneless skinless chicken breast cut into ¼ inch strips
1 tablespoon water
1 ½ teaspoon vinegar
1 ½ teaspoon splenda
Dash hot pepper sauce
½ cup Walnut halves
3 tablespoons olive oil
1 medium green pepper cut into 1 inch pieces
½ teaspoon ground ginger
Hot cooked brown rice

In a bowl, combine 1 teaspoon of cornstarch and 1 tablespoon light soy sauce stir until smooth, add chicken and toss to coat. Cover and refrigerate for 30 minutes. Meanwhile in a bowl combine water, vinegar, splenda, hot pepper sauce, remaining cornstarch and soy sauce. Set aside. In a skillet sauté walnuts in oil until toasted, remove with a slotted spoon and set aside. In the same skillet stir fry chicken until juices run clear. Remove and keep warm, add green pepper and ginger to skillet. Cook and stir for 3 minutes or until pepper is crisp tender. Stir cornstarch mixture, add to skillet. Bring to a boil. Cook and stir for 2 minutes or until thickened and bubbly. Return chicken and walnuts to pan. Serve over brown rice.
4 servings

Chicken & Dumplings

4 cups fat free chicken broth
½ cup sliced celery
½ cup peas
½ cup sliced carrots
1 bay leaf
1 teaspoon dried parsley flakes

Dumplings
2 cups Bisquick Reduced fat mix
¼ teaspoon dried thyme
Dash ground nutmeg
2/3 cup skim milk
½ teaspoon dried parsley flakes
3 cups cubed cooked chicken breast

Gravy
¼ cup all purpose flour
½ cup water
¼ teaspoon salt
1/8 teaspoon pepper

In a 5 quart broiler combine broth, peas, carrots, bay leafs and parsley bring to a boil. For dumplings combine biscuit mix, thyme and nutmeg, stir in milk and parsley just until moistened. Drop by tablespoonfuls onto the boiling broth. Cook uncovered for 10 minutes cover and cook 10 minutes longer with a slotted spoon remove dumplings to a serving dish, keep warm. Place broth in a sauce pan bring to a boil combine, flour, water, salt and pepper until smooth gradually stir into broth. Cook and stir over medium heat until thickened about 2 minutes. Pour over chicken and dumplings
4 servings.

Baked Mushroom Chicken

4 boneless skinless chicken breast halves (1 pound)
¼ cup all purpose flour
3 tablespoons light butter divided
1 cup sliced fresh mushrooms
½ cup fat free chicken broth
¼ teaspoon salt
1/8 teaspoon pepper
1/3 cup shredded mozzarella cheese
1/3 cup grated parmesan cheese
¼ cup sliced green onion

Flatten each chicken breast half to ¼ inch thickness. Place flour in a reseable plastic bag. Add Chicken a few pieces at a time. Seal and shake to coat. In a large skillet brown chicken in 2 tablespoons, butter on both sides. Transfer to a greased baking dish. In the same skillet, sauté mushrooms in the remaining butter until tender. Add the broth, salt, pepper. Bring to a boil. Cook for 5 minutes or until liquid is reduced to ½ cup spoon over chicken. Bake uncovered at 375 degrees for 15 minutes sprinkle with the cheese and green onion. Bake 5 minutes longer or until the chicken juices run clear.
4 servings.

Chicken with Cherry Sauce

1 pound fresh or frozen pitted sweet cherries
½ cup orange juice
½ cup light soy sauce
¼ cup brown splenda
¼ cup honey
2 tablespoons lemon juice
1 garlic clove minced

½ teaspoon ground ginger
1 broiler/fryer chicken (3 to 4 pounds) cut up

Set aside ¾ cup cherries. In a blender combine orange juice and remaining cherries, cover and process until smooth. Add the soy sauce, brown splenda, honey, lemon juice, garlic, and ginger set aside. In a large skillet over medium heat, brown chicken on all sides in butter place chicken skin side down on an ungreased baking dish. Top with cherry sauce. Bake uncovered at 350 degrees for 20 minutes turn chicken. Top with reserved cherries. Bake uncovered 25–30 minutes or until chicken pieces run clear.
4–6 servings

Wrapped Garlic Chicken

4 boneless skinless chicken breast halves
4 large sheets aluminum foil
½ teaspoon salt
1 cup sliced mushrooms
1 can Healthy Choice Cream of Roasted Garlic Condensed Soup
4 sprigs fresh rosemary or 1 cup dry rosemary leaves

Place 1 chicken breast in center of each sheet of foil. Sprinkle with salt. Top each with mushroom, soup and rosemary. Fold foil in half over chicken, seal all edges with double foil seals. Bake 425 degrees for 20 minutes or until chicken is no longer pink in center.
4 servings

Cheesy Chicken Rice Bake

1 bag uncooked Success brown rice (3/4 cup)
1 can (10 ¾ oz) Campbell's condensed Cream of Chicken soup (98% fat free)

1 cup water
½ teaspoon onion powder
¼ teaspoon ground black pepper
4 to 6 boneless chicken breast halves
1 cup shredded cheddar cheese

Mix rice, soup, water, onion powder and black pepper in 2 quart shallow baking dish. Top with chicken sprinkle with cheese and additional black pepper. Cover and bake at 375 degrees for 45 minutes or until chicken is no longer pink and rice is done, uncover and sprinkle with additional cheese.
4–6 servings

Crunchy Chicken Fingers

1 tablespoon Canola Oil
4 ½ cups corn flakes
½ teaspoon onion powder
1 ¼ teaspoons salt
½ teaspoon pepper
½ cup all purpose flour
2 pounds boneless skinless chicken breast tenderloins
2 eggs beaten
Ketchup optional

Preheat oven to 425 degrees. Line large baking pan with foil, brush with oil. In a bowl combine cereal, onion powder, ½ teaspoon salt and ¼ teaspoon pepper. In a separate bowl combine flour with remaining salt and pepper coat chicken with flour mixture shaking off excess. Dip into egg coat with cereal mixture place on pan. Coat chicken with cooking spray. Bake until golden and cooked through 15–20 minutes. Serve with ketchup if desired.
6 servings

Pork

Orange Pork Chops

6 Pork Chops (1/2 inch thick)
1 tablespoon olive oil
1 can (11 oz) mandarin oranges drained
½ teaspoon ground cloves
Pepper to taste

In a skillet brown pork chops on both sides in olive oil. Top with oranges sprinkle with cloves and pepper, cover and simmer for 35 minutes or until meat juices run clear.
6 servings

Tender Pork Ribs

¾ to 1 cup vinegar
½ cup ketchup
2 tablespoon splenda
2 tablespoon light Worcestershire sauce
1 garlic clove minced
1 teaspoon ground mustard
1 teaspoon paprika
½ to 1 teaspoon salt
1/8 teaspoon pepper
2 pounds pork spareribs
1 teaspoon olive oil

Combine the first nine ingredients in a slow cooker. Cut ribs into serving size pieces. Brown in a skillet in oil. Transfer to slow cooker cover and cook on low for 4–6 hours or until tender.
2–3 servings

Tender Pork Chops

½ cup all purpose flour
2 teaspoon salt
1 ½ teaspoon ground mustard
½ teaspoon garlic powder
6 pork loin chops (3/4 inches thick) trimmed
2 tablespoon olive oil
1 can (10 ¾ oz) condensed Healthy choice cream of chicken soup undiluted
¾ cup water

In a shallow bowl, combine flour, salt, mustard and garlic powder dredge pork chops. In a skillet brown the chops on both sides in oil place in a slow cooker combine soup and water pour over chops cover and cook on low for 6–8 hours or until meat is tender. If desired thicken pan juices and serve with the pork chops
6 servings.

Pork Chops & Apples

6 boneless pork loin chops (1 inch thick)
1 tablespoon olive oil
1 package (6 oz) whole wheat stuffing mix
1 can (21 oz.) light apple pie filling with cinnamon

In a skillet, brown pork chops in oil over medium heat. Prepare stuffing according to package directions. Spread pie filling into a greased baking

pan. Place the pork chops on top, spoon stuffing over chops, cover and bake at 350 degrees for 35 minutes. Uncover bake 10 minutes longer.
6 servings

Cherry Pork Chops

4 boneless pork chops (1 inch thick)
1 tablespoon olive oil
1 cup orange juice
¾ cup pitted sweet cherries halves
2 green onions sliced
¼ cup no sugar cherry preserves
4 tablespoons cornstarch
3 tablespoons cold water

In a large skillet brown pork chops in oil on both sides, drain. Add the orange juice, cherries and onion to skillet bring to a boil. Reduce heat simmer, uncovered for 15 minutes turning the chops twice. Remove chops and keep warm. Stir preserves into pan juices. In a bowl combine the cornstarch and cold water until smooth, stir into pan juices. Bring to a boil cook and stir for 1–2 minutes or until thickened. Serve over chops,

Applesauce Pork Loin

1 boneless pork loin roast (3 pounds)
½ teaspoon salt
¼ teaspoon pepper
2 tablespoon olive oil
1 cup unsweetened applesauce
3 tablespoon Dijon mustard
1 tablespoon honey
3 fresh rosemary sprigs

Sprinkle roast with salt and pepper. In a large skillet brown roast on all sides in oil. Place on a rack in a shallow roasting pan. Combine the applesauce, mustard and honey spread over roast. Top with rosemary. Bake uncovered at 350 degrees for 1 to 2 ½ hours. Let stand for 10 minutes before slicing.
10–12 servings

Maple Glazed Pork Chops

½ cup all purpose flour
salt and pepper to taste
4 bone in pork loin chops (1inch thick)
2 tablespoons light butter
¼ cup cider vinegar
1/3 cup maple syrup
1 tablespoon cornstarch
3 tablespoon water
2/3 cup brown splenda

In a large resealable plastic bag combine flour, salt and pepper. Add pork chops and shake to coat. In a skillet, brown chops on both sides in butter. Place in an ungreased 13 x 9 x 2 inch baking pan. Bake uncovered at 450 degrees for 20–25 minutes or until juices run clear. Meanwhile in a skillet bring the vinegar to a boil reduce heat. Add Maple syrup cover and cook for 10 minutes combine cornstarch and water until smooth, add to the maple mixture. Bring to a boil cook and stir for 2 minutes until thicken. Place chops on a broiler pan sprinkle with brown splenda. Broil 4 inches from the heat for 2–3 minutes or until splenda is melted. Drizzle with maple glaze.
Serves 4

Pork Chops with Mustard Crumbs

3 tablespoon olive oil
1/3 cup coarse rye bread crumbs (2 to 3 slices)
2 garlic cloves minced
1 tablespoon finely chopped fresh sage or ½ teaspoon dried sage
½ teaspoon salt
¼ teaspoon black pepper
4 (3/4 to 1 inch thick pork chops 2 lb total)
2 tablespoon Dijon mustard

Preheat oven to 425 degrees. Heat 2 tablespoon oil in a 10 inch heavy skillet over moderately high heat then sauté bread crumbs, garlic, sage, salt and pepper stirring until crumbs are golden brown 3 to 5 minutes. Transfer crumbs to a bowl and clean skillet. Pat Pork dry. Heat remaining tablespoon oil in skillet over moderately high heat then brown chops in batches, turning over once about 4 minutes. Transfer chops to a baking pan and spread with mustard and then bread crumbs. Roast in middle of oven until meat is just cooked through 5 to 7 minutes
4 servings

Pork Chops Parmesan

Vegetable oil spray
2 tablespoons all purpose flour
1 large egg
2 slices whole wheat bread
1 tablespoons parsley
¼ cup shredded parmesan cheese
1 teaspoon basil
½ teaspoon thyme
½ teaspoon oregano
1 teaspoon garlic powder

1 teaspoon olive oil
¼ teaspoon pepper
4 boneless center cut pork chops

Preheat the oven to 375 degrees. Lightly spray an 8 inch square baking pan with vegetable oil spray. Put the flour and egg in two separate bowls. In a food processor chop until the bread is crumbs. Put the mixture into a bowl. Coat the pork chops with the flour shaking off the excess coat it with the egg then with the bread crumb mixture. Place in the baking pan. Repeat with the remaining pork chops. Bake for 45 minutes or until the pork is no longer pink in the center

Beef

Bacon Topped Meat Loaf

2 eggs lightly beaten
1 tablespoon Worcestershire sauce
1 medium onion chopped
1 cup (4 oz. 2% milk shredded cheddar cheese)
2/3 cup whole wheat bread crumbs
½ teaspoon salt
¼ teaspoon pepper
2 pounds lean ground beef
2 bacon strips halved

In a bowl combine the first seven ingredients. Crumble beef over mixture and mix well. Shape into a loaf in an ungreased baking dish. Top with bacon. Bake uncovered at 350 degrees for 1 hour or until meat is no longer pink. Let stand for 10 minutes before cutting.
8 servings

Herbed Roast Beef

When I cook this for Sunday Dinner and my son walks in he says I know what we are having for dinner Mom's wonderful roast.

Bone in beef roast (4 to 6) pounds
2 teaspoons dried rosemary crushed
2 teaspoons each dried basil, marjoram and thyme
2 teaspoons rubbed sage

1 medium onion sliced
6 fresh rosemary sprigs
1 ½ cup (12 oz.) light sour cream
¼ cup prepared horseradish sauce
2 tablespoon snipped chives
5 tablespoon lemon juice

Trim Roast. In a small bowl, combine the crushed rosemary, basil marjoram, thyme and sage rub over roast. Place with fat side up on a rack in a roasting pan. Top with onions and rosemary sprigs. Bake uncovered at 350 degrees for 2 ½ to 3 ½ hours. Discard onion and rosemary. Let roast stand for 10–15 minutes before slicing. Meanwhile in a small bowl combine the sauce ingredients. Serve with beef.
10–12 servings

Peppercorn Steak

1 tablespoon whole black peppercorn crushed
2 boneless beef strips
2 to 3 tablespoons light butter
1 to 2 garlic cloves minced
1 tablespoon Worcestershire sauce
½ cup no fat beef broth
1 teaspoon slenda
2 tablespoon cornstarch
1 tablespoon water

Rub pepper over both sides of steak. Refrigerate for 15 minutes. In a ungreased skillet over medium high heat brown steaks on both sides. Add butter and garlic cook for 4–6 minutes, turning once or until meat reaches desired doneness. Remove steaks keep warm. Combine broth and splenda add to the pan stir to loosen browned bits combine corn-

starch and water stir until smooth. Bring to a boil cook and stir for 2 minutes or until thickened. Serve with the steak.
2 servings

Grilled Sirloin Steak

1 cup light soy sauce
¼ cup cider vinegar
¼ cup olive oil
1 tablespoon garlic salt
1 tablespoon ground ginger
1 tablespoon honey
1 boneless beef sirloin steak

In a large resealable plastic bag. Combine the first six ingredients add beef. Seal bag and turn to coat refrigerate for at least 3 hours or overnight. Drain and discard the marinade. Grill steak covered over medium heat 1 ½ to 2 hours.
6 servings

Roast Beef and Gravy

1 (3 pound boneless beef chuck roast)
2 (10 ¾ oz) 98% fat free cream of mushroom soup
1/3 cup 99% fat free beef broth
1 envelope onion soup mix

Place all ingredients in a slow cooker and cook on low for 8–9 hours or on high for 4–5 hours.

Sirloin Steak with Golden Onions

1 ½ lb. Boneless sirloin steak fat trimmed
½ teaspoon each salt and pepper
3 medium onions sliced ¼ inch thick

Horseradish sauce
½ cup reduce fat sour cream
2 teaspoon each prepared horseradish and sliced scallions
¼ teaspoon each pepper and splenda

Cook steak and onions in a large nonstick skillet sprayed with nonstick spray, cook on medium high heat sprinkle steak with salt and pepper. Scatter onions around steak. Cook over medium high heat, turning steak once and stirring onion often. Cook 12 minutes or until steak is medium rare and onions are golden and tender, Transfer steak to cutting board let stand 5 minutes. Meanwhile stir horseradish sauce ingredients in a small bowl to combine. Slice steak and onions and serve with the horseradish sauce.
Serves 4

Cheesteak Pasta

8 oz whole wheat pasta
2 cups 2% milk cheddar cheese
2 teaspoons cornstarch
1 teaspoon Dijon mustard
¼ teaspoon paprika
1 cup 2% milk
1 ½ cup reserved cooked sirloin steak cut in narrow strips
1 cup reserved cooked onion chopped
1 cup diced tomatoes
Garnish chopped parsley

Cook and drain pasta as package directs. Meanwhile whisk milk and cornstarch in a medium saucepan to blend. Bring to a boil over medium high heat, stirring often. Whisk in mustard and paprika simmer 1 minute or until thickened. Add cheese steak and onion. Stir until cheese melts. Remove from heat toss with pasta. Top with the tomatoes sprinkle with parsley.
Serves 4

Beef Stroganoff

1 pound of lean ground beef
1 bag whole wheat noodles
1 small container of light sour cream
1 can of healthy request cream of mushroom soup
½ cup of 2% milk
salt and pepper to taste

Boil the noodles(about ¾ of a pack if it is a small bag) Brown the ground beef in a skillet and drain the grease. Combine entire can of soup with ½ cup of milk. Stir together in a skillet on low heat. Add sour cream. Once it has thickened add the beef. Pour over drained noodles.

Salisbury Steak

1 (10 3/4 oz.) can health choice mushroom soup, undiluted and divided
1 ½ pounds lean ground beef
½ cup finely chopped onion
¼ cup Italian-seasoned breadcrumbs
1 large egg, beaten
1 ½ cups sliced fresh mushrooms
1/3 cup fat free beef broth

¼ cup Worcestershire sauce
¼ teaspoon pepper

Combine ¼ cup soup, beef and next 3 ingredients; stir well. Shape mixture into 6 (1/2 inch thick) patties.
Brown patties in large skillet over medium-high heat. Remove patties, discarding half of pan drippings. Cook mushrooms in remaining drippings in skillet over medium high heat, stirring constantly, until tender. Combine remaining soup, beef broth, Worcestershire sauce and pepper add to mushroom mixture. Return patties to skillet; bring to boil. Cover reduce heat and simmer 20 minutes.
Yield 6 servings

Creamy Beef Strips

1 ½ pounds round steak
2 tablespoons olive oil
salt and pepper to taste
1 medium onion sliced
1 (3 or 4 oz) can of mushrooms
¾ cup fat free beef broth
1 cup light sour cream
¼ teaspoon dry mustard

Cut round steak into strips and brown in oil, sprinkle lightly with salt and pepper. Add sliced onion, drained mushrooms and dry mustard. Cook until mushrooms are browned and onion is tender. Add beef broth cover and simmer about an hour or until meat is tender. Remove meat mixture from heat add sour cream mix well.

Turkey

Turkey with Gravy

1 bone in turkey breast 5 to 6 pounds
1 medium onion quartered
1 tablespoon lemon pepper
1 ½ teaspoon garlic powder
1 ½ teaspoon onion powder
1 teaspoon paprika
2 teaspoons all purpose flour
1 cup water
1 chicken bouillon cube

Combine all ingredients and place in crock pot. Add turkey breast and cook on low for 5–6 hours or until done.

Saucy Turkey

2 tablespoons light butter
1 small onion chopped
1 small green pepper chopped
1 cup ketchup
½ cup fat free chicken broth
1 ½ teaspoon Worcestershire sauce
1 teaspoon prepared mustard
¼ teaspoon hot pepper sauce
¼ teaspoon pepper

3 cups cubed cooked turkey
Brown rice cooked

In a large saucepan melt butter sauté onion and green pepper until tender. Stir in ketchup, broth, Worcestershire sauce, mustard, hot pepper sauce and pepper. Add turkey simmer uncovered for 20 minutes or until heated through. Serve over cooked brown rice.
4 servings

Turkey Bake

4 cups cooled stuffing
2½ cups cubed cooked turkey
2 cups cooked broccoli florets
1 cup carrots cooked
2 cups turkey gravy
4 slices 2% milk sharp cheddar cheese.

Press the stuffing onto the bottom of a greased 2 ½ quart baking dish. Layer the other ingredients as listed on top of the stuffing, Cook until heated through.
4 servings

Turkey Breast

1 lb turkey cutlets
2 teaspoon lemon pepper
2 teaspoon lemon juice
1 teaspoon light Worcestershire sauce
1 teaspoon Dijon mustard
1 teaspoon parsley

Coat a large skillet with cooking spray heat for 30 seconds. Add turkey sprinkle with lemon pepper and cook for 3 to 5 minutes on each side until browned and no longer pink in center. Combine remaining ingredients in a small bowl, mixing well. Add to pan and cook until heated through garnish with lemon and parsley.

Turkey Meatloaf

1 ½ lbs ground turkey
1 package (12 oz) soy veggie crumbles thawed if frozen
1 small onion finely chopped ½ cup
½ cup Italian seasoned dry breadcrumbs
½ cup shredded fat free cheddar cheese (2 oz)
½ cup ketchup
1 egg
2 teaspoons chopped parsley
2 teaspoons Worcestershire
2 cloves garlic minced
½ teaspoon salt
¼ teaspoon pepper

Preheat over to 375 degrees. Coat 9x5 loaf pan with cooking spray. Combine turkey, crumbles, onion, breadcrumbs, cheese, ¼ cup ketchup, egg, ¼ cup water, 1 ½ teaspoon parsley, 1 teaspoon Worcestershire, garlic, salt and pepper transfer to pan. Bake 30 minutes. Combine remaining ketchup and Worcestershire, Brush half of mixture over meat loaf. Bake 15 minutes, brush remaining ketchup mixture over loaf. Bake until cooked through sprinkle with parsley
8 servings.

Fish

Shrimp with Noodles

6 oz. Egg noodles
1 envelope herb and garlic soup mix
1 ¾ cups skin milk
1 pound uncooked shrimp peeled and divined
2 cups broccoli florets
¼ cup grated parmesan cheese

Cook egg noodles according to package directions. Meanwhile combine soup mix and milk in a saucepan cook and stir over medium heat until smooth. Add shrimp and broccoli simmer uncovered for 3–5 minutes or until shrimp are no longer pink. Drain pasta. Toss with the shrimp mixture Sprinkle with parmesan cheese.
4 servings

Tarragon Salmon

2 salmon Steaks (about 1 inch thick)
2 tablespoons light butter melted
2 teaspoons lemon juice
1 teaspoon dried basil
1 tablespoons minced fresh tarragon
1 tablespoon minced fresh parsley
½ teaspoon onion salt
salt and pepper to taste

Place the salmon steaks in an greased baking dish. Drizzle with the tarragon, parsley, basil, pepper, salt and onion salt. Bake uncovered at 350 degrees for 20–25 minutes
2 servings

Grilled Salmon

½ cup light butter
1/3 cup lemon juice
2 tablespoon minced parsley
1 ½ teaspoon light soy sauce
1 teaspoon dried oregano
½ teaspoon garlic powder
1/8 teaspoon pepper
¼ teaspoon salt
1 salmon fillet (2 ½ to 3 pounds and ¾ inch thick)

In a saucepan, combine the first 8 ingredients, cook and stir over low heat until butter is melted, set aside. Coat grill rack with nonstick cooking spray before starting grill. Place salmon skin side down on grill. Grill over medium hot heat for 5 minutes. Baste with butter sauce. Grill 10–15 minutes longer or until fish flakes easily with fork.
6–8 servings

Catfish Ginger Sauce

½ cup chopped green onion
1 tablespoon canola oil
¼ teaspoon ground ginger
1 teaspoon cornstarch
2 tablespoon water
1 cup fat free chicken broth

1 tablespoon light soy sauce
1 tablespoon white wine vinegar
1/8 teaspoon cayenne pepper
4 catfish fillets (6 oz each)

In a 2 cup microwave, safe bowl combine onion and ginger microwave uncovered on high for 1 ½ minutes or until the onions are tender. In a small bowl combine the cornstarch and water until smooth. Add broth, soy sauce, vinegar and cayenne mix well, stir into onion mixture. Microwave uncovered at 70% power for 3–4 minutes stirring after each minute until sauce comes to a boil. Place catfish in a microwave safe 3 quart casserole pour sauce over the fish. Cover and microwave on high for 6–7 minutes.
4 servings

Stewed Salmon

1 medium onion diced
4 tablespoon light butter
1 (14 ¼ oz) can salmon
1 ½ cups water
½ teaspoon salt
½ teaspoon pepper
½ teaspoon accent

In a large skillet, sauté the onion in butter until tender. Turn the salmon out of the can saving the liquid. Pick the salmon free of bones. Add the salmon and its liquid along with the water to the skillet add salt and pepper and accent and simmer for 10 minutes serve hot over brown rice.

Shrimp with Rice

Two 6 oz. Boxes Uncle Ben's long-grain and wild rice
2 pounds shrimp, cleaned, peeled, and divined
1 onion diced and sautéed in 2 tablespoons light butter
1 bell pepper chopped
Two 10 ¾ ounce cans condensed light cream of mushroom soup
16 ounces 2% milk grated Cheddar cheese; reserve ½ cup for top
1 tablespoon Worcestershire sauce
½ teaspoon dry mustard

Remove seasoning mix from rice; do not use. Cook rice as directed on box. Preheat oven to 375 degrees. Mix rice with remaining ingredients in a baking dish and sprinkle reserved cheese on top. Bake for 45 minutes.

Quick Tuna Casserole

1 can Healthy Choice cream of celery soup
1 can water
¼ teaspoon salt
Dash of pepper
1 ½ cups Brown Minute Rice (dry)
1 can green peas drained
1–10 oz can tuna drained and flaked
½ cup grated 2% milk cheddar cheese

In saucepan, combine soup, water, salt, pepper and peas. Bring to boil. Remove from heat; stir in rice and tuna. Pour into greased 2 quart casserole. Sprinkle with grated cheese. Bake at 350 degrees about 20 minutes or until rice has absorbed liquid. Do not bake dry.

Southern Jambalaya

1 pound large shrimp, shelled and divined
1 green bell pepper, cut into strips
1 can (14 ½ oz.) whole tomatoes undrained
1 can (10 ½ oz.) condensed fat free chicken broth
2 tablespoons Cayenne Pepper Sauce
½ teaspoon dried thyme leaves
1 1/3 cups uncooked instant brown rice
1 1/3 cups French Fried Onions, Divided

Generously spray large nonstick skillet with nonstick cooking spray. Add shrimp cook about 3 minutes or until shrimp are opaque.
Stir in bell pepper, tomatoes with liquid, chicken broth, pepper sauce, thyme, rice and 2/3 cup French Fried Onions. Bring to a boil stirring occasionally. Cover; remove from heat. Let stand 5 to 8 minutes or until all liquid is absorbed. Sprinkle with remaining 2/3 cup onions just before serving.
Makes 6 servings

Deserts

PIES

Lemon Meringue Pie

6 Tablespoons corn starch
1 cup of splenda
½ teaspoon salt
2 cups boiling water
3 egg yolks
¼ cup lemon juice
2 teaspoons butter

Combine corn starch, splenda, salt then add 2 cups boiling water. Cook until thick and transparent stirring constantly. Add egg yolk slightly beaten into a little of the hot water mixture, blend and return to pan. Cook about 2 minutes longer stirring constantly. Blend in lemon juice, butter and grated lemon rind. Cool before turning into bake pie shell.

Meringue
3 egg whites
¼ teaspoon cream of tartar
3 tablespoons splenda

Preheat the oven to 350 degrees. Beat the egg whites with the cream of tartar until they form soft peaks. Add 1 tablespoon of splenda at a time beating constantly until the whites form stiff peaks. Spoon the meringue over the pie filling spreading it out to touch the crust all around. Bake until brown 10 to 12 minutes. Note: For meringue use 1 tablespoon splenda for each egg white.

Coconut Cream Pie

¾ cup splenda
¼ teaspoon salt
3 slightly beaten egg yolks
1 teaspoon vanilla
1/3 cup all purpose flour
2 cups 2% milk
2 tablespoon light butter
1 cup flaked coconut
1–9 inch baked pie shell

Meringue
3 egg whites
¼ teaspoon cream of tartar
3 tablespoon splenda

Filling
In a saucepan combine splenda, flour and salt gradually stir in milk. Cook and stir over medium heat until mixture boils and thickens. Remove from heat, add egg yolks. Mix well and return to heat for 2 minutes stirring constantly. Remove from heat and add butter and vanilla and coconut and mix well. Pour the filling into the crust. Spoon the meringue over the pie filling spreading it out to touch the crust all around. Bake until brown 10 to 12 minutes.

Chocolate Pie

1 cup Splenda
2 ½ heaping teaspoons of cocoa
1 ½ cups of 2% milk
1 teaspoon vanilla
2 heaping tablespoons flour
3 egg yolks
½ stick light butter
1 baked pie shell

Preheat oven to 350 degrees. Mix splenda, flour and cocoa. Add eggs, milk, butter and vanilla. Cook until slightly thickened. Pour into pie shell. Spread meringue on top and bake in oven until meringue is slightly browned 10 to 12 minutes.

Fresh Strawberry Pie

3 pints fresh whole strawberries
1 baked pie crust

Clean berries drain and fill crust

Filling
1 cup Splenda
3 tablespoons sugar free strawberry jello
1 cup water
3 tablespoons cornstarch
1 to 2 drops of red food coloring.

Mix together in sauce pan and bring to a boil. Boil for 45 seconds. Pour over berries and chill 3 hours or overnight. Top with lite cool whip before serving.

Apple Pie

6 to 7 cooking apples
½ cup splenda
½ teaspoon nutmeg
½ teaspoon cinnamon

Wash apples and quarter, core and slice. Spread half the sliced apples in even layer in pastry lined pie plate. Sprinkle with half the splenda mixture. Dot with ½ teaspoon butter. Repeat layers, using remaining apples and splenda mixture. Dot with ½ teaspoon butter. Cover with reserved top crust trim even with bottom crust, fold edges under together cut a few slits in top of crust to allows steam to escape. Bake 10 minutes at 425 degrees reduce heat to moderate (350 degrees) and bake 30 to 45 minutes longer or until apples are just tender. Remove from oven. Serve hot or cold. Makes 1–9 inch pie.

Sweet Potato Pie

A true southern favorite.

1 ¼ cups of splenda
½ teaspoon ground cinnamon
½ teaspoon nutmeg
2 eggs
1 cup fat free evaporated milk
1 teaspoon vanilla extract
1 ½ cups mashed cooked sweet potatoes
1 unbaked pie crust

In a mixing bowl blend splenda and spices beat eggs add milk and vanilla. Stir in potatoes. Beat until smooth. Pour into pie shell. Bake at 425 degrees for 15 minutes. Reduce heat to 350 degrees and bake for an

additional 30 minutes. Cool. Store in refrigerator. Serve with Light Cool Whip.
6–8 Servings

Double Layer Pumpkin Pie

4 ounces light cream cheese softened
1 tablespoon fat free evaporated milk
1 tablespoon splenda
1 ½ cups light cool whip
1 light graham cracker pie crust
1 cup fat free evaporated milk
2 packages (4 oz serving size) sugar free vanilla instant pudding
1 can (16oz.) pumpkin
1 teaspoon ground cinnamon
½ teaspoon ground ginger
¼ teaspoon ground cloves

Soften cream cheese in microwave on high 15 to 20 seconds. Mix milk, splenda and cream cheese in large bowl with wire whisk until smooth. Gently stir in light cool whip topping spread on bottom of crust. Pour 1 cup milk into bowl add pudding mix. Beat with wire whisk until well blended 1 to 2 minutes(mixture will be thick) Stir in pumpkin and spices with wire whisk, mix well. Spread over cream cheese layer refrigerate at least 2 hours. Garnish with additional cool whip. Makes 8 servings

Easy Pumpkin Pie

1 Deep Dish Pie Crust
2 eggs
1 can (16 oz) solid pack pumpkin
1 can (12oz) fat free evaporated milk

¾ cup Splenda
3 teaspoon pumpkin pie spices

Preheat oven and baking sheet to 375 degrees. In a large bowl, using a wire whisk, whisk together eggs, pumpkin, milk, splenda and spice. Pour filling into frozen crust. Bake on preheated baking sheet 30 minutes. Serves 8

No Bake Banana Cream Pie

5 tablespoons fat free caramel ice cream topping
1 prepared reduce fat graham cracker crust
3 bananas sliced (3 cups)
2 packages instant sugar free fat free vanilla pudding mix
2 ½ cups fat free milk
1 container (16 oz) light cool whip

Spread 3 tablespoons caramel topping over bottom of crust top with half of bananas. In bowl whisk dry pudding mix and milk until smooth and thick, 2 minutes. Gradually fold 2 cups whipped topping into pudding. Spread half of pudding mixture over bananas in crust. Top with remaining bananas spread with remaining pudding mixture. Refrigerate until set. About 2 hours top with remaining cool whip drizzle with caramel.

Charaman's Pecan Pie

1 cup brown splenda
¼ cup lite butter
3 eggs
1 cup light corn syrup
¼ teaspoon lite salt

1 teaspoon vanilla
1 ½ cups coarsely broken pecan meats

Cream butter and splenda. Add eggs and beat well. Add syrup, salt and vanilla. Mix well. Stir in pecans by hand. Pour into 9 or 10 inch unbaked pie shell. Place in oven preheated to 450 degrees and reduce to 350 degrees. Bake until cracks appear in filling. Filling will be firm when cooled.

Fresh Blueberry Pie

¾ cup Splenda
3 tablespoon cornstarch
1/8 teaspoon light salt
¼ cup cold water
5 cups fresh blueberries divided
1 tablespoon light butter
1 tablespoon lemon juice
1 baked pie crust

In a saucepan over medium heat combine splenda, cornstarch, salt and water until smooth. Add 3 cups blueberries bring to a boil, cook and stir for 2 minutes or until thickened and bubbly. Remove from the heat add butter, lemon juice and remaining berries, stir until butter is melted. Cool pour into the pastry shell refrigerate.
6–8 servings.

Chocolate Ribbon Pie

4 oz package fat free cream cheese softened
1 ½ cups skim milk divided
1 teaspoon splenda

2 cups thawed cool whip light divided
1 reduced fat graham cracker crumb crust (6 oz)
1 package (4 serving size) chocolate flavor fat free sugar free instant pudding & pie filling mix

Beat cream cheese, 1 teaspoon of the milk and splenda in medium bowl with electric mixer on medium speed until well blended. Gently stir in ½ cup of the whipped topping. Spread into bottom of crust. Pour remaining milk into large bowl. Add dry pudding mix. Beat with wire whisk 2 minutes or until well blended spread over cream cheese layer. Refrigerate 4 hours or until set just before serving spread remaining 1 ½ cup whipped topping over pudding layer
8 servings

Chocolate Meringue Pie

My daughter is a chocoholic and this is one of her favorite pies.

2 tablespoons flour
2 tablespoons corn starch
½ teaspoon salt
½ cup splenda
1 square chocolate
2 cups of 2% milk
2 eggs separated
3 teaspoons of vanilla

Meringue
3 egg whites
¼ teaspoon cream of tartar
3 tablespoon splenda

Blend together flour, corn starch, salt and splenda, add chocolate and milk. Cook until thickened stirring constantly. Add slightly beaten egg yolks(to prevent lumping first blend a little of the hot mixture with the egg yolks.) Cook one minute longer. Add vanilla. Pour into baked pie shell cover with meringue. Return to slow oven 325 degrees to brown.

Georgia Peach Pie

After all Georgia is called the Peach state.

1 unbaked pie crust
4 large peaches
3/4 cup splenda blend
1/3 cup self rising flour
2 eggs well beaten
½ stick light butter
¼ teaspoon almond flavoring

Peel and slice peaches put into pie shell. Mix splenda, flour, eggs, butter and flavoring combine well and pour over peaches. Bake 350 degrees until crust is brown and filling is thick.

Puddings

Southern Banana Pudding

My daughter can make better Banana Pudding than I can and this is her recipe.

¾ cup splenda blend divided
1/3 cup flour
Dash lite salt
3 eggs separated
2 cups skim milk
½ teaspoon vanilla
45 Reduced Fat Vanilla wafers
5 medium ripe bananas sliced

Preheat over to 350 degrees. Mix ½ cup of the splenda, flour and salt in top of double boiler. Blend in 3 egg yolks and milk. Cook uncovered, over boiling water 10 to 12 minutes or until thickened, stirring constantly. Remove from heat, stir in vanilla.
Reserve 12 of the wafers for garnish. Spread small amount of custard on bottom of 1-1/2 quart baking dish, cover with layers of 1/3 each of the remaining wafers and sliced bananas. Pour about 1/3 of the remaining custard over bananas. Continue to layer wafers, bananas and custard to make a total of 3 layers of each ending with custard.

Beat egg whites on high speed of electric mixer until soft peaks form. Gradually add remaining ¼ cup splenda blend, beating until stiff peaks form. Spoon over custard, spread evenly to cover entire surface of custard and sealing well to edge.

Bake 15 to 20 minutes or until lightly browned. Cool slightly. Top with reserved 12 wafers just before serving.
Makes 12 servings

Rice Pudding

2 cups cooked rice
2 cups skin milk
½ cup brown splenda
2 eggs
1 teaspoon vanilla
¼ teaspoon salt
½ cup seedless raisins
cinnamon or nutmeg

Preheat over to 350 degrees. Beat brown splenda, eggs, vanilla and salt to blend. Slowly stir scalded milk into egg mixture. Blend in cooked rice and raisin. Pour into 1 ½ quart casserole set in pan containing 1 inch hot water. Bake 55 minutes or until a knife inserted in center comes out clean. Remove from oven and sprinkle with cinnamon or nutmeg before serving.
6 servings

Blueberry Pudding

2 cups fresh or frozen blueberries
1 teaspoon ground cinnamon
1 teaspoon lemon juice
1 cup all purpose flour
¾ cup splenda
1 teaspoon baking powder
½ cup skim milk
3 tablespoon light butter melted

Topping
¾ cup splenda
1 tablespoon cornstarch
1 cup boiling water

Toss the blueberries with cinnamon and lemon juice. Please in a greased 8 inch square baking dish. In a bowl combine flour, splenda and baking powder stir in milk, butter. Spoon over berries combine splenda and cornstarch, sprinkle over batter. Slowly pour boiling water over all. Bake at 350 degrees for 45–50 minutes or until the pudding test done.
Servings 9

Desert

Walnut Apple Desert

8 cups sliced peeled tart apples (6 medium)
2 teaspoon ground cinnamon
1 cup light butter
2 eggs
2 cups all purpose flour
1 cup finely chopped walnuts divided
2 ½ cup splenda divided
Sugar free ice cream

Place apples in a greased 13 inch x 9 inch x 2 inch baking dish. Sprinkle with ¼ cup splenda and cinnamon. In a mixing bowl cream butter and remaining splenda, add eggs. Stir in flour and ½ cup walnuts. Spread over apples. Sprinkle with remaining walnuts. Bake at 350 degree for 45–55 minutes or until the apples are tender. Serve warm with sugar free ice cream.
12–16 servings

Easy Cobbler

1 stick light butter
2 cups fruit
1 cup splenda
1 cup skim milk
1 cup reduced fat baking mix

Melt butter. Combine fruit and splenda and add to butter. Pour into 1 ½ quart round casserole dish. Combine milk and biscuit baking mix and pour over fruit. Bake at 400 degree for 40 minutes.

Cakes

Cocoa Angel Food Cake

12 egg whites
¾ cup cake flour
1 ½ cups splenda blend divided
¼ cup baking cocoa
1 teaspoon cream of tarter
¼ teaspoon salt

Let egg whites stand at room temperature for 30 minutes. Sift the flour, ½ cup splenda and cocoa together five times set aside. In a mixing bowl beat egg whites, cream of tarter and salt on high speed until soft peaks form. Add the remaining splenda 2 tablespoons at a time, beating well after each addition. Gradually fold in sifted dry ingredients. Spoon into an ungreased 10 inch tube pan bake at 350 degrees for 35–40 minutes or until the top springs back when lightly touched and feels dry immediately invert pan cool completely. Loosen sides of cake from pan and remove.
12 servings

German Chocolate Cake

This is my daughter's favorite.

1 package (4 oz) Baker's German Sweet Chocolate
½ cup boiling water
1 cup light butter
2 cups splenda blend

4 egg yolks
1 teaspoon vanilla
2 ½ cups sifted cake flour
1 teaspoon baking soda
½ teaspoon salt
1 cup lite buttermilk
4 egg white stiffly beaten

Melt chocolate in boiling water cool. Cream Butter and splenda until fluffy. Add yolks one at a time beating well after each. Blend in vanilla and chocolate. Stir flour with soda and salt add alternately with buttermilk to chocolate mixture, beating after each addition until smooth. Fold in beaten whites. Pour into three 9 inch layer pans, lined on bottoms with wax paper. Bake at 350 degrees for 30 to 35 minutes cool. Frost with Coconut Pecan Frosting

Coconut Pecan Frosting

Combine 1 cup light evaporated milk, 1 cup splenda blend, 3 slightly beaten egg yolks, ½ cup light butter and 1 teaspoon vanilla. Cook and stir over medium heat until thickened about 12 minutes. Add 1 ½ cups coconut and 1 cup chopped pecans. Cool until thick enough to spread beating occasionally. Makes 2 ½ cups

Fresh Ellijay, Georgia Apple Cake

Every year we go to the apple festival in Ellijay, GA and bring back plenty of apples to make this wonderful cake.

2 cups plain flour
1 ½ teaspoon baking soda
½ teaspoon salt
1 teaspoon cinnamon

2 cups splenda blend
2 eggs
1 ½ cups canola oil
2 teaspoon vanilla
1 cup chopped nuts
5 cups finely chopped apples

Sift flour, soda, salt and cinnamon together, beat eggs and splenda until creamy. Add canola oil and vanilla and beat until smooth, add sifted flour mixture and mix to form stiff dough. Stir in apples and nuts. Pour into a greased and floured 10 inch tube pan. Bake at 300 degrees for 1 hour.

Glaze

2 tablespoon light butter
1 tablespoon all purpose flour
1/8 teaspoon salt
¼ cup 2% milk
¼ cup brown splenda
¼ teaspoon vanilla
1 cup splenda blend

Melt butter in a saucepan. Blend in flour and salt. Add milk all at once, stirring constantly. Bring to a boil cook and stir until thick and bubbly. Remove from the heat, beat in brown splenda and vanilla. Add splenda mix until smooth. Drizzle over cake.
Servings 12

Yellow Cake

1 cup splenda Blend for Baking
3 cups cake flour
2 teaspoon baking powder

½ teaspoon baking soda
¾ cup light butter
1 ¼ cup buttermilk divided
3 egg yolks
2 teaspoon vanilla extract

Preheat oven to 350 degrees. Lightly grease and flour 2 eight inch cake pans. Set aside. Mix splenda, flour, baking powder and baking soda together in a medium bowl stir until well blended cut butter into chunks. Add to flour mixture. Mix at medium speed until mixture is crumbly in appearance (about one minute) Pour ¼ cup buttermilk into the flour mixture mix at low speed until blended, Blend remaining buttermilk, egg yolks and vanilla together in a small bowl. Add ½ of the mixture to the flour mixture. Mix at medium high speed until well blended (about 30–45 seconds) scrape sides of bowl add the remaining milk mixture. Mix until well blended. Scrape sides of bowl and mix again if necessary to remove any lumps spoon batter evenly into prepare pans. Bake for 35–40 minutes.

Fluffy Chocolate Frosting

1 cup cold skin milk
1 package (3.9 oz.) chocolate no sugar instant pudding mix
1 carton (8 oz) lite cool whip

In a mixing bowl beat the milk and pudding mix for 2 minutes. Beat in cool whip topping. Spread over cake refrigerate any left overs.

Fresh Coconut Cake

I make this cake every Christmas. It is a tradition around our house.

1 fresh coconut
½ cup splenda blend for baking

3 cups cake flour
2 teaspoon baking powder
½ teaspoon baking soda
¾ cup light butter
1 ¼ cup buttermilk divided
4 egg yolks
2 teaspoon vanilla extract

Preheat oven 350 degrees. Lightly grease and flour 2 eight inch cake pans. Set aside. Mix splenda, flour, baking powder and baking soda together in a medium bowl stir until well blended cut butter into chunks. Add to flour mixture. Mix at medium speed until mixture is crumbly in appearance (about one minute). Pour ¼ cup buttermilk into the flour mixture mix at low speed until blended, Blend remaining buttermilk, egg yolks and vanilla together in a small bowl. Add ½ of the mixture to the flour mixture. Mix at medium high speed until well blended (about 30–45 seconds) scrape sides of bowl add the remaining milk mixture. Mix until well blended. Scrape sides of bowl and mix again if necessary to remove any lumps spoon batter evenly into prepare pans. Bake for 35–40 minutes or until toothpick inserted in center comes out clean, cool for 15 minutes on rack before removing from pans. Drill holes in a fresh coconut drain the milk into a cup. Remove one layer from pan and slowly spoon ½ of the milk over the layer. Frost with 7 Minute Coconut Frosting and sprinkle with coconut. Then put the second layer on top of frosted layer and slowly spoon rest of coconut milk over layer, frost and sprinkle with coconut.

7 Minute Coconut Frosting

1/3 cup light white corn syrup
1/2 cup splenda
1 teaspoon cream of tarter
3 tablespoon of water
2 eggs white

In a double boiler mix together and beat with electric mixture till stiff. Spread icing on layers and sprinkle with coconut.

Hummingbird Cake

3 cups all purpose flour
1 cup splenda blend for baking
1 teaspoon baking soda
1 teaspoon cinnamon
½ teaspoon salt
3 eggs beaten
¾ cup canola oil
1 ¾ cup mashed bananas
1 (8oz) can crushed pineapple in own juice
1 cup chopped pecans
1 ½ teaspoon vanilla extract

Preheat oven to 350 degrees grease and flour three 9 inch round cake pans. In a mixing bowl stir together the flour, Splenda Blend for Baking, baking soda, cinnamon and salt. Add the eggs and oil and stir just until the dry ingredients are moistened. Stir in the bananas, the pineapple and its juice, the pecans and the vanilla. Divide the batter among the prepared pans and bake for 23 to 28 minutes or until a wooden pick inserted in the center comes out clean. Cool the cake layers in the pan for 10 minutes then turn them out on to a rack to cool.

7 Minute Frosting

1/3 cup light white corn syrup
1/2 cup splenda
1 teaspoon cream of tarter
3 tablespoon of water
2 eggs white

In a double boiler mix together and beat with electric mixture till stiff.

Spice Cake

½ cup light butter
½ cup brown splenda
3 eggs separated
1 teaspoon vanilla extract
1 ¾ cup cake flour
½ teaspoon allspice
1 teaspoon baking soda
1 teaspoon cinnamon
1 teaspoon cloves
½ teaspoon salt
1 cup (8oz) light sour cream

Frosting
¼ cup brown splenda
1/3 cup water
2 eggs white
¼ teaspoon cream of tartar
1 ½ teaspoon vanilla extract

In a large mixing bowl cream butter and brown splenda. Beat in the egg yolks and vanilla. Combine the dry ingredients. Add to creamed mixture alternately with sour cream. In a small mixing bowl beat egg whites until stiff. Gently fold into batter. Pour into greased and floured 9 inch round baking pans. Bake at 350 degrees for 25–30 minutes. Cool for 10 minutes before removing from pans.

For Frosting
In a heavy saucepan bring brown splenda and water to a boil. Boil 3–4 minutes or until a candy thermometer reads 242 degrees beat egg whites and cream of tartar until foamy. Gradually add hot splenda mixture,

beat on high for 7 minutes or until stiff peaks form add vanilla continue beating until frosting reaches desired consistency about 2 minutes spread between layers and over top and sides of cake. Sprinkle with cinnamon and walnuts. Refrigerate any leftovers
12–16 servings

Applesauce Cake

1 cup water
1 cup raisins
1 cup diced dried fruit
2 cups all purpose flour
½ cup splenda
1 ½ teaspoon cinnamon
1 teaspoon baking soda
½ teaspoon salt
½ teaspoon ground nutmeg
2 eggs
1 cup unsweetened apple sauce
½ cup canola oil
1 teaspoon vanilla extract
½ cup chopped nuts

In a saucepan bring water to a boil add raisins and dried fruit then remove from heat. Let stand for 10 minutes drain well and set aside. In a bowl combine the flour, splenda, cinnamon, baking soda, salt and nutmeg. In another bowl combine the eggs, applesauce, oil and vanilla until blended stir into the dry ingredients until well blended. Fold in nuts and fruit pour into a 10 inch fluted tube pan coated with nonstick cooking spray. Bake at 325 degrees for 35–40 minutes or until a toothpick inserted near the center of the cake comes out clean. Cool in pan for 10 minutes before removing
16 servings

Glaze
2 tablespoons light butter
1 tablespoons all purpose flour
1/8 teaspoon salt
¼ cup skim milk
¼ cup brown splenda
¼ teaspoon vanilla extract
1 cup splenda
chopped walnuts

Melt butter in a saucepan. Blend in flour and salt. Add milk all at once, stirring constantly. Bring to a boil cook and stir until thick and bubbly. Remove from the heat beat in brown splenda and vanilla. Add splenda and beat until smooth. Drizzle over cake sprinkle with nuts
12 servings

Carrot Cake

2 cups flour
2 teaspoon baking powder
1 ½ teaspoon baking soda
1/3 teaspoon light salt
2 teaspoon cinnamon
1 cup splenda blend for baking
1 cup canola oil
4 eggs
2 cups grated carrots
6 oz can crushed pineapple drained
½ cup chopped nuts
3 ½ oz can coconut

Sift dry ingredients together in a large bowl. Add splenda, oil, eggs and mix well. Add carrots, nuts, coconut and pineapple and blend well. Bake in 10 inch tube pan at 350 degrees for one hour.
16 servings

Frosting

In a quart saucepan over medium heat. Heat 1 ½ cups splenda, 1 cup lite butter, 1 cup low fat buttermilk, 2 teaspoons light corn syrup and 1 teaspoon baking soda to boiling stirring constantly until small amount of mixture dropped in cold water forms soft ball. Pour mixture into large bowl with mixer at high speed beat icing until spreading consistency, about 7 minutes, occasionally scraping bowl with rubber spatula. Fold in 1 cup finely chopped pecans.

Red Velvet Cake

This is a great cake for Christmas.

¾ cups splenda blend for baking
2 ½ cups plain cake flour
1 cup buttermilk
1 teaspoon soda
2 eggs
1 ½ cups canola oil
1 teaspoon vanilla
1 teaspoon vinegar
1–5/8 oz bottle red food coloring

Beat eggs, add splenda, cooking oil and vinegar. Sift cake flour and soda together. Add milk slowly. Add flavoring and cake coloring. Grease and line two 9-inch cake pans. Pour batter into prepared pans and bake in a pre-heated oven at 350 degrees for 30 minutes.

Fluffy White Frostings

½ cup splenda blend for baking
1/3 cup light corn syrup
3 tablespoon water
3 egg whites
1 teaspoon vanilla extract

Combine splenda, syrup and water in small saucepan. Stir and heat to boiling over medium heat, boil without stirring until reaches 240 on candy thermometer(soft ball stage) as syrup boils beat egg whites with electric mixer until stiff. Pour hot syrup very slowly into eggs whites, beating constantly, add vanilla and beat several minutes or until stiff.

Pineapple Upside-Down Cake

½ cup light butter
½ cup brown splenda
3 (8 ½ oz) cans pineapple slices undrained
10 pecan halves
11 maraschino cherries halved
2 large eggs, separated
1 egg yolk
½ cup splenda blend
1 cup all purpose flour
1 teaspoon baking powder
½ teaspoon ground cinnamon
¼ teaspoon lite salt
1 teaspoon vanilla extract
¼ teaspoon cream of tartar

Melt butter in a 10 inch cast-iron skillet over low heat. Sprinkle brown splenda in skillet. Remove from heat.

Drain pineapple, reserving ¼ cup juice. Set juice aside. Cut pineapple slices in half, reserving 1 whole slice.

Place whole pineapple slice in center of skillet. Arrange 10 pineapple pieces spoke fashion around whole slice in center of skillet. Place a pecan half and a cherry half between each piece of pineapple. Place a cherry half in center of whole pineapple slice.

Arrange remaining pineapple pieces, cut side up, around sides of skillet. Place a cherry half in center of each piece of pineapple around sides of skillet.

Beat 3 egg yolks at high speed with an electric mixer until thick and pale; gradually add 1 cup splenda; beating well. Combine flour and next 3 ingredients; stir well. Add to egg mixture alternately with reserved ¼ cup pineapple juice. Stir in vanilla.

Beat egg whites and cream of tartar at high speed until stiff peaks form; fold beaten egg whites into batter

Spoon batter evenly over pineapple in skillet. Bake at 350 degrees for 45 to 50 minutes or until cake is set. Invert cake onto a serving plate. Scrape any remaining glaze from skillet onto cake. Cut into wedges to serve

8 servings

Chocolate Pound Cake

2 cups splenda blend
¼ cup canola oil
2 sticks light butter
5 eggs
3 cups plain flour
½ teaspoon salt
½ teaspoon baking powder
½ cup cocoa
1 ¼ cup 1% milk
2 teaspoons vanilla

Cream splenda, canola oil and butter add eggs one at a time mixing well. Sift dry ingredients and stir into butter and egg mixture. Pour into a greased tube pan and bake at 325 degrees for 1 ½ hours.

Chocolate Icing
1 cup splenda blend
2 tablespoons cocoa
2 eggs
4 tablespoons light cream.

Bring to a rolling boil set off and cool and beat until desired consistency.

Pound Cake

This is my Mother's pound cake recipe.

1 ½ cups light butter
1 ¼ cups splenda
8 eggs
¼ teaspoon salt
3 cups plain flour
1 teaspoon vanilla flavoring
1 teaspoon lemon flavoring
1 teaspoon almond flavoring

Mix all ingredient well. Pour into a greased tube pan and bake at 325 degrees for 1 ½ hours.

Do Nothing Cake

2 cups all purpose flour
2 eggs slightly beaten

½ teaspoon salt
1 (20oz) can crushed pineapple, undrained
1 cup splenda blend for baking
1 teaspoon vanilla
1 teaspoon baking soda

Combine all ingredients and mix by hand. Do not use an electric mixer. Pour into greased 9x12 inch pan. Bake at 350 degrees for 30 to 35 minutes.

Topping
1 (15oz) can fat free evaporated milk
½ cup splenda blend for baking
½ cup light butter

Mix milk, splenda, and butter in a medium saucepan. Boil for 5 minutes. Spread over warm cake.
Yield 12 servings

Chocolate Chip Cake

1 cup chopped dates
1 teaspoon baking soda
1 cup boiling water
½ cup light butter
¾ cup splenda blend for baking divided
2 lightly beaten eggs
1 ½ cups all-purpose flour
2 tablespoons cocoa
½ teaspoon salt
1 teaspoon vanilla
½ cup coarsely chopped pecans
½ package (6 oz) semisweet chocolate chips

Combine dates, baking soda and boiling water. Set aside to cool. Cream butter, ½ cup splenda and eggs. Sift flour, cocoa and salt. Add flour mixture alternately with date mixture. Add vanilla. Grease 8x8 inch square cake pan. Pour in batter. Sprinkle nuts, chocolate chips and remaining splenda over top. Bake at 350 degrees for 40 minutes or until no crumbs stick to toothpick when inserted into the center of the cake.
Yield 8 servings

Caramel Apple Cake with Caramel Topping

1 ¼ cups splenda blend for baking
3 eggs
1 ½ cups canola oil
3 cups all-purpose flour
2 teaspoons vanilla
1 cup chopped pecans
2 ½ cups diced apples, canned or fresh

Preheat over to 350 degrees. Cream together splenda, eggs, and oil. Add flour, mix together until well blended. Add vanilla, nuts, and diced apples. Spread into a lightly greased and floured 13 x 9 inch baking dish; bake for 45 to 60 minutes. Cake is done when toothpick inserted in center comes out clean. When cake is done, punch holes in it with a knife and pour topping over.

Caramel Topping
¾ pound (3 sticks) butter
½ cup brown splenda for baking
¼ cup 1% milk

Heat all ingredients together over medium heat. Bring to boil, stirring constantly. Let boil for about 2 minutes. Pour over warm cake.

Pineapple Cake

One 16 ounce can crushed pineapple in its own juice
2 cups reduced fat biscuit mix
1 cup sifted all purpose flour
1 teaspoon baking soda
½ cup splenda blend for baking
¾ cup light sour cream
8 tablespoons (1 stick) light butter
2 teaspoons vanilla
2 large eggs
2 tablespoons rum extract

Preheat oven to 350 degrees. Drain pineapple well reserving juice for glaze. Stir biscuit mix, flour and baking soda together and set aside. Beat sour cream, butter, and vanilla together for 2 minutes. Add eggs and beat 1 additional minute. Add flour mixture and beat 1 minute longer. Mix in drained pineapple and rum extract. Pour into well greased 9 inch Bundt pan. Bake for about 45 minutes or until cake tests done. Remove from oven and spoon about half the glaze over cake. Let stand 10 minutes and then turn onto serving plate. Spoon on remaining glaze. Cool before cutting.

Glaze

¾ cups splenda blend for baking
4 tablespoons lite butter
¼ cup reserved pineapple juice
2 tablespoons rum extract

Combine splenda, butter and pineapple juice. Stir over low heat until splenda is dissolved and butter is melted. Remove from heat and add rum extract.

Old-Time Lemon Cheesecake

I remember my Mother making this cake and it is just as good as I remember.

1 ½ sticks light butter
2 cups splenda blend for baking
3 ½ cups all purpose flour
3 ½ teaspoons baking powder
1 cup 1% milk
1 teaspoon vanilla
6 egg whites beaten to stiff peaks

Preheat oven to 375 degrees. Cream butter, add splenda. Sift flour and baking powder together three times and add to butter alternately with milk and vanilla. Fold in egg whites. Bake in three greased 8 inch round pans for 35 minutes.

Icing

9 egg yolks
¾ cups splenda blend for baking
¾ pound (3 sticks) light butter
juice and zest of 4 lemons

Mix all ingredients together and cook in double boiler until thick, approximately 20 minutes. Allow cake to cool. Spread icing in between layers and on entire outside of cake.

Sweet Potato Cake

2/3 cup light butter
1 cup splenda blend for baking

4 large eggs, separated
1 cup mashed, cooked sweet potato
2 cups all purpose flour
1 teaspoon ground all spice
1 teaspoon ground cinnamon
1 teaspoon ground cloves
1 teaspoon ground nutmeg
1 cup light buttermilk
1 teaspoon vanilla extract
1 ½ cups raisins
2 cups chopped pecans

Beat butter at medium speed with an electric mixer until creamy; gradually add 1 cup splenda, beating well. Add egg yolks one at a time, beating after each addition. Add sweet potato to mixture, mixing well.
Combine flour and next 7 ingredients; add to butter mixture alternately with buttermilk, beginning and ending with flour mixture. Mix at low speed after each addition until blended. Stir in vanilla, raisins and pecans. Beat egg whites at high speed until stiff peaks form; fold into batter. Spoon batter into a greased and floured 10 inch tube pan.
Bake at 325 degrees for 1 hour and 25 to 30 minutes or until wooden pick inserted in center comes out clean. Cool in pan on a wire rack 10 minutes; remove from pan and cool completely on wire rack. Sprinkle with powdered sugar, if desired.
Yield 16 servings.

The Compromise Cake

This cake is a compromise of a fruit cake.

1 ½ cups applesauce
1 ½ teaspoons baking soda
1 cup raisins

1 cup chopped dates
1 cup chopped pecans
½ cup light butter
¾ cup splenda blend
1 teaspoons vanilla extract
2 large eggs
2 cups sifted cake flour
2 tablespoons unsweetened cocoa
½ teaspoon salt
½ teaspoon ground cinnamon
½ teaspoon ground cloves
½ teaspoon ground nutmeg

Grease a 10 inch tube pan; line bottom of pan with wax paper. Set aside. Combine applesauce and soda; let stand 10 minutes. Combine raisins, dates and pecans; set mixture aside.
Beat butter at medium speed with an electric mixer until fluffy; gradually add splenda beating well. Add vanilla and eggs, one at a time, beating after each addition.
Combine flour and remaining 5 ingredients. Add ½ flour mixture to raisin mixture; toss gently, and set aside. Gradually add remaining flour mixture to butter mixture mixing well. Add applesauce mixture and raisin mixture mixing well.
Pour batter into prepared tube pan. Bake at 350 degrees for 30 minutes. Reduce temperature to 325 degrees, and bake 30 more minutes or until a wooden pick inserted in center of cake comes out clean. Cool cake in pan on a wire rack 15 minutes; remove from pan and peel off wax paper. Cool completely on wire rack.
Yield 24 servings.

Cookies

Chocolate Chip Cookies

My daughter loves anything with chocolate and these cookies are no exception.

2 ½ cups all purpose flour
1 teaspoon baking soda
1 teaspoon salt
1 cup light butter
¼ cup splenda
¼ cup brown splenda
1 teaspoon vanilla extract
2 large eggs
1 package (12 oz.) semi-sweet chocolate morsels

Combine flour, baking soda and salt in a small bowl set aside. Beat butter, splenda, brown splenda and vanilla at medium speed with an electric mixer until blended. Add eggs one at a time mixing well after each addition. Scrape sides of bowl. Gradually add flour mixture beating until blended. Stir in chocolate morsels spoon rounded tablespoon of cookie dough onto ungreased baking sheets. Preheat oven to 375 degrees. Bake cookies 9 to 11 minutes or until lightly browned.
Make 3 dozen cookies.

Pecan Cookies

2 sticks light butter
4 tablespoons splenda
2 cups chopped pecans
2 cups sifted plain flour
3 teaspoon vanilla extract

Cream butter and splenda, add flour, then vanilla. Add nuts and mix well. Roll into 2 or 3 rolls in wax paper. Chill slice with knife when ready to use. Bake at 350 degrees on ungreased cookie sheet about 15 minutes or until lightly browned.

Peanut Butter Cookies

¼ cup creamy or crunchy reduced fat peanut butter
¼ light butter softened
¼ cup splenda
1 egg beaten
¾ cup all purpose flour
¼ teaspoon salt
¼ teaspoon soda
¼ cup brown splenda

Blend peanut butter, light butter and splenda in a medium mixing bowl. Add egg, mixing well. Stir in flour, salt and soda add more flour if dough is not stiff enough to shape into a roll about 2 ½ inches thick. Wrap in waxed paper and chill overnight. Cut into slices ¼ inch thick. Bake at 350 degrees for 10 minutes. Makes about 2 ½ dozen.

Peanut Oatmeal Cookies

1 cup light butter
½ cup splenda
½ cup brown splenda
2 eggs
1 teaspoon vanilla
1 ½ cups sifted plain flour
½ teaspoon soda
3 cups quick cooking oats
½ pound salted Spanish peanuts

Cream butter, add splenda, eggs and vanilla beat until light and fluffy. Add remaining ingredients. Mix well. Drop by teaspoon onto greased cookie sheet. Bake in 375 degree oven about 10 minutes.

Chocolate Chip & Walnut Cookies

½ cup quick cooking oats
2 ½ cups all purpose flour
1 ½ teaspoon baking soda
½ teaspoon light salt
¼ teaspoon cinnamon
1 cup (2 sticks) light butter
½ cup brown splenda
½ cup splenda
2 teaspoon vanilla extract
1 teaspoon lemon juice
2 eggs
3 cups semisweet chocolate chips
1 ½ cups chopped walnuts

Combine oats, flour, baking soda, salt and cinnamon in a mixing bowl. In another bowl cream butter, splenda, and brown splenda, vanilla and lemon juice together using an electric mixer. Add eggs and beat until fluffy. Stir the flour mixture into egg mixture, blending well. Add the chocolate chips and nuts to the dough and mix well using ¼ cup of dough for each cookie scoop rounds balls with an ice cream scoop and place 2 ½ inches apart on baking sheets. Preheat oven to 350 degrees. Bake until cookies are lightly brown 16–18 minutes.
Makes 2 dozen cookies.

Drop Sugar Cookies

2 cups all purpose flour sifted
2 teaspoons baking powder
½ teaspoon light salt
2 large eggs
½ cup splenda plus additional splenda for topping
2/3 cup Canola oil
2 teaspoon vanilla extract
1 teaspoon grated lemon zest

Sift flour, baking powder and salt into a medium bowl and mix well. Whisk eggs in a large bowl until blended. Add splenda, oil, vanilla extract and lemon zest and mix well. Stir the dry ingredients into egg mixture until blended. Chill, covered for 30 minutes or longer. Preheat the oven to 400 degree. Drop the cookie dough by rounded teaspoonfuls 2 inches apart onto ungreased baking sheets. Mist the bottom of a 3 inch flat bottom glass in additional splenda. Press the top of each cookie lightly with glass to flatten. Bake cookies until lightly browned. About 8 minutes. Cool on baking sheets for 2 minutes. Remove to wire racks to cool.
Makes 4 dozen cookies.

Macadamia Nut Cookies

1 cup light butter softened
½ cup splenda
½ cup brown splenda
2 eggs
1 teaspoon vanilla extract
2 ¼ cups all purpose flour
1 teaspoon baking soda
1 teaspoon light salt
2 jars (3 ½ oz. Jar Macadamia nuts chopped)
2 cups (12 oz semisweet chocolate chips)
1 cup vanilla or white chips

In a mixing bowl cream butter and splenda. Add eggs and vanilla, beat on medium speed for 2 minutes combine flour baking soda and salt add to creamed mixture and beat for 2 minutes. Stir in nuts and chips. Cover and refrigerate several hours or overnight. Drop by tablespoonful 2 inches apart onto ungreased baking sheets. Bake at 375 degrees for 10–12 minutes or until golden brown. Cool on pan for 1 minute before removing.
Makes about 6 dozen.

Southern Tea Cakes

This is a very old Southern recipe. I remember my Grandmother making these for all her Grandchildren.

4 cups all-purpose flour
1 teaspoon baking soda
2 teaspoon baking powder
1 cup splenda
2 eggs

½ cup buttermilk
½ pound light butter softened
1 teaspoon vanilla

Preheat oven to 350 degrees. In a large bowl sift flour, baking soda, and baking powder together. Add remaining ingredients and blend well. Dough should be soft. Roll dough out onto a floured surface until approximately ¼ inch thick. Cut dough into desired shapes and bake on a slightly greased sheet for 10 to 12 minutes
Yields 6 to 8 dozen.

Thumb Print Cookies

¾ pound (3 sticks) light butter, softened
½ cup splenda
2 egg yolks
3 ¾ cups all purpose flour
¼ teaspoon lite salt
1 teaspoon vanilla
Any tart sugar free preserves (plum for example)

Cream butter and splenda. Add egg yolks. Sift flour and salt, blend into butter mixture. Add vanilla. Chill dough thoroughly. Preheat oven to 350 degrees. Shape dough into 1 inch balls and place on an ungreased cookie sheet. Make indentation in center of each with thumb; fill with preserves. Bake for 15 minutes or until lightly browned. Cool slightly remove to rack to finish cooling. These keep well in a tightly closed container.

Caramel Squares

1 stick light butter
½ cup brown splenda

1 egg
1 cup self-rising flour
1 cup pecans chopped

Cream butter and splenda. Add egg. Stir in flour and nuts. Bake in 9x9 inch pan at 350 degrees for 25 to 30 minutes.
Yield: 12 servings

Ice Box Cookies

½ cup brown splenda
1 egg slightly beaten
½ teaspoon baking soda
½ teaspoon vanilla
½ cup light butter
2 cups plain flour
½ teaspoon cream of tartar
½ cup finely chopped pecans

Cream splenda and eggs together. Add the rest of the ingredients. Make into about 9 inch rolls approximately 1 ½ inches in diameter. Wrap in wax paper and place in refrigerator at least 8 hours. Cut real thin. Bake at 350 degrees until brown.
Yield: 42 to 48 cookies.

Banana Oatmeal Cookies

1/2 cup splenda
1 cup light butter
2 eggs
1 teaspoon vanilla extract
2 cups all purpose flour
1 teaspoon baking soda

1 teaspoon ground cloves
1 teaspoon ground cinnamon
3 medium ripe bananas mashed
2 cups quick cooking oats
1 cup (6 ounces) semisweet chocolate chips

In a large bowl cream splenda, butter, eggs and vanilla. Combine flour, baking soda, cloves and cinnamon; add to creamed mixture. Stir in bananas, oats and chocolate chips. Drop by round teaspoonfuls onto greased cookie sheets. Bake at 375 degrees for 10–12 minutes. Immediately remove cookies to wire racks to cool.
Yield: about 4 dozen

Coconut Macaroons

1 1/3 cup flaked coconut
1/4 cup splenda
2 egg whites
2 tablespoons all purpose flour
½ teaspoon vanilla extract
1/8 teaspoon light salt

Combine all ingredients; stir well. Drop by level tablespoonfuls onto a greased cookie sheet. Bake at 350 degrees for 20 minutes; remove to a wire rack cool. Yield 1 dozen

Forgotten Cookies

Preheat oven to 350 degree

2 egg white—stiffly beaten
Pinch of light salt
¼ cup of splenda (add 1 tablespoon at a time)

1 teaspoon vanilla
1 cup chopped pecans
1 cup chocolate chips

Beat egg whites till stiff. Add salt and splenda 1 tablespoon at a time while beating. Add vanilla. Fold in nuts and chips. Place 1 inch apart on foil covered cookie sheets.

Place in preheated oven. Turn off oven and Forget several hours or overnight. Store in airtight container.

Pastel Cookies

3 ½ cups flour
1 teaspoon Calumet Baking Powder
1 ½ cups (3 sticks) light butter or margarine
½ cup Splenda
1 package (4-serving size) of sugar free gelatin, any flavor
1 egg
1 teaspoon vanilla
Additional gelatin any flavor

Heat oven to 400 degrees

Mix Flour and baking powder in medium bowl. Beat butter in large bowl with electric mixer to soften. Gradually add splenda and 1 package of sugar free gelatin, beating until light and fluffy. Beat in egg and vanilla. Gradually add flour mixture, beating well after each addition.

Shape dough into 1-inch balls. Place on ungreased cookie sheets Flatten with bottom of glass. Sprinkle with additional gelatin.

Bake 10 to 12 minutes or until edges are lightly browned. Remove from cookie sheets. Cool on wire racks. Store in tightly covered container.
Makes about 5 dozen cookies

Lemon Sugar Cookies

3 cups unsifted flour
2 teaspoons baking powder
½ teaspoon light salt
1 cup splenda
1 cup light butter
2 eggs
¼ cup lemon juice

Preheat over to 350 degrees. Stir together flour, baking powder and salt; set aside. In large mixing bowl, beat splenda and lite butter until fluffy; beat in eggs. Stir in dry ingredients, then lemon juice; mix well. Chill 2 hours. Shape into 1 ¼ inch balls; roll in additional splenda. Place 2 inches apart on greased baking sheets; flatten. Bake 8 to 10 minutes or until lightly browned.
Makes about 8 dozen

Brownies

1 cup splenda
1 ¾ cups all purpose flour
½ cup baking cocoa
1 teaspoon lite salt
5 eggs
1 cup canola oil
1 teaspoon vanilla
1 cup (6 oz.) semisweet chocolate chips

In a mixing bowl, combine the first seven ingredients. Beat until smooth. Pour in a greased 13x 9 inch baking pan. Sprinkle with chocolate chips. Bake at 350 degrees for 30 minutes.

Breads

Banana Bread

My daughter made this and took it in to her office. Everyone loved it. She says the cream cheese is the secret.

1–8 ounce package of light cream cheese, softened
1 cup Splenda
¼ cup light butter
1 cup mashed ripe banana
2 eggs
2 ¼ cups flour
1 ½ teaspoons baking powder
½ teaspoon baking soda
1 cup chopped nuts

Combine cream cheese, splenda and margarine, mixing until well blended. Blend in banana and eggs. Add remaining ingredients, mixing until moistened. Pour into greased and floured 9x5 inch loaf pan. Bake 350 degrees, 1 hour and 10 minutes or until wooded pick inserted near center comes out clean. Cool 5 minutes; remove from pan. Serve with additional cream cheese if desired.
1 loaf

Carrot Bread

2 cups plain sifted flour
2 teaspoon baking soda

2 teaspoons cinnamon
½ teaspoon salt
1 ½ cups splenda
1 cup Canola oil
½ cup flaked coconut
½ cup chopped nuts
2 cups grated raw carrots
3 eggs well beaten
2 teaspoons vanilla

Stir together Canola oil and splenda until smooth. Sift together flour, soda, cinnamon and salt, stir flour mixture into splenda and oil alternate with eggs. Add carrots, coconut, nuts and vanilla. Pour into a well greased loaf pan. Let stand 20 minutes. Bake 1 hour in a 350 degree oven cool in pan at least 10 minutes.

Date Nut Bread

1 pound pitted Dates
1 teaspoon baking soda
1 ½ cups boiling water
1/3 cup softened light butter
1 ½ cups splenda
2 eggs beaten
¼ teaspoon light salt
1 teaspoon vanilla
3 ½ cups all purpose flour
1 cup chopped walnuts

Put chopped dates in a large mixing bowl. Sprinkle soda over dates and pour boiling water over all. Stir well and let sit until cool. Beat butter and splenda together until light, add eggs, salt and vanilla and beat well add to dates and beat vigorously. Stir in flour a small amount at a time.

Stir in nuts. Spoon batter into two oiled 8 inch loaf pans and bake at 300 degrees for 1 hour. 2 loaves.

Bacon Walnut Bread

3 cups biscuit mix
1 cup 2% milk
2 eggs beaten
2 tablespoons dried onion
¾ cup cheddar cheese shredded made with 2% milk
12 slices of turkey bacon cooked and crumbled
½ cup chopped walnuts

In a large bowl, combine the biscuit mix, milk, eggs and onion just until moistened. Stir in cheese, bacon and walnuts. Spread into a greased loaf pan. Bake at 350 degrees for 48–52 minutes or until a tooth pick inserted near the center comes out clean. Cool for 10 minutes before removing from pan.
1 loaf

Angel Rolls

3 ½ cups bread flour divided
1 tablespoons splenda blend
1 package (1/4 ounce) quick rise yeast
1 ¼ teaspoon light salt
1 ¼ teaspoon baking powder
½ teaspoon baking soda
1 cup warm low fat buttermilk (120 degrees to 130 degrees)
½ cup Canola oil
1/3 cup warm water (120 degrees to 130 degrees)
Light butter melted

In a mixing bowl, combine 1 ½ cups flour, splenda, yeast, salt, baking powder and baking soda. Add the buttermilk, oil and water, beat until moistened. Stir in enough remaining flour to form a soft dough. Turn onto a floured surface and knead until smooth and elastic about 4–6 minutes. Cover and let rest for 10 minutes. Roll out to ½ inch thickness. Cut with a 2 ½ inch biscuit cutter. Place on a greased baking sheet. Bake at 400 degrees for 15–18 minutes or until golden brown. Brush tops with butter 14 rolls. Note: Warm buttermilk will appear curdled.

Whole Wheat Rolls

2 packages (1/4 ounce each) active yeast
½ cup light butter melted
1/3 cup honey
3 cups whole wheat flour
1 teaspoon light salt
2 cups warm low fat buttermilk (110 degrees to 115 degrees)
1 teaspoon baking soda
1 ½ to 2 ½ cups all purpose flour

In a mixing bowl, dissolve yeast in warm buttermilk. Add the butter, honey, whole wheat flour, salt and baking soda. Beat until smooth. Stir in enough all purpose flour to form a soft dough. Turn onto a floured surface. Knead until smooth and elastic. About 6–8 minutes. Place in a greased bowl, turning once to grease top cover and let rise in a warm place until doubled about 1 hour. Punch dough down. Turn onto a lightly floured surface divide into seven portions. Divide each portion into six pieces, shape each into a ball. Place 2 inches apart on greased baking sheets cover and let rise in a warm place until doubled about 30 minutes. Bake until golden brown.

Easy Dinner Rolls

1 cup warm water (105 degrees to 115 degrees)
2 packages active dry yeast
½ cup light butter
½ cup splenda
3 eggs
1 teaspoon light salt
4–4 ½ cups unbleached all purpose flour.
Additional melted butter optional

Combine the warm water and yeast in a large bowl. Let the mixture stand until yeast is foamy, about 5 minutes. Stir in butter, splenda, eggs and salt. Beat in flour 1 cup at a time until dough is too stiff to mix (some flour may not be needed) cover and refrigerate 2 hours or up to 4 days. Grease a 13x9 inch baking pan. Turn the chilled dough out onto a lightly floured board. Divide dough into 24 equal size pieces. Roll each piece into a smooth round ball. Place balls in even rows in the prepared pan. Cover and let dough balls rise until doubled in volume about 1 hour, preheat oven to 375 degrees. Bake until rolls are golden brown. 15–20 minutes. Brush warm rolls with melted butter if desired.

Low Fat Biscuits

2 ¼ cups reduced fat biscuit mix
¾ cup fat free(skim) milk

Stir ingredients until soft dough forms. Turn onto surface dusted with biscuit mix. Knead 10 times. Roll dough ½ inch thick. Cut with 2 ½ inch cutter. Place on ungreased cookie sheet. Bake 7–9 minutes or until golden brown
9 biscuits.

Cheese Biscuits

2 cups reduced fat biscuit mix
1 cup low fat buttermilk
¾ cup shredded fat free cheddar cheese
1 teaspoon splenda
1/3 cup light butter

Preheat oven to 350 degrees. Mix flour, baking powder, and splenda together. Using a fork cut in butter until it resembles cornmeal. Add cheese. Stir in buttermilk all at one time just until blended. Do not over stir. Drop tablespoonfuls onto a well greased baking sheet. Bake for 12 to 15 minutes.

Finger Rolls

1 package dry yeast
1 cup warm water (105 degrees to 115 degrees)
1 tablespoon splenda
1 tablespoon canola oil
1 ½ teaspoon salt
3 to 3 ½ cups all purpose flour
½ cup lite butter melted and divided

Dissolve yeast in warm water in a large bowl let stand 5 minutes. Add splenda, oil, salt and 1 ½ cups flour. Beat at medium speed with an electric mixer 2 minutes. Stir in enough flour to make a soft dough. Turn dough out onto a lightly floured surface and knead until smooth and elastic (3 to 4 minutes). Place dough in a well greased bowl, turning to greased top. Cover and let rise in a warm place (85 degrees) free from drafts 1 hour or until doubled. Pour ¼ cup butter into a 13 x 9 x2 inch baking pan set aside. Shape dough into 20 (1 ¼ inch balls, shape each ball into a 4x1/2 inch roll. Place rolls in prepared pan cover and let rise

30 minutes. Lightly brush rolls with remaining ¼ cup butter. Bake at 400 degrees for 18 to 20 minutes or until lightly browned makes 20 rolls.

Italian Dinner Rolls

1 cup 2% milk
3 tablespoons light butter
2 tablespoons splenda
1 ½ teaspoon Italian seasoning
1 teaspoon light salt
2 packages dry yeast
½ cup warm water (105 degrees to 115 degrees)
2 eggs
4 ½ cups all purpose flour divided
½ cup grated parmesan cheese
2 tablespoons butter melted
Additional grated parmesan cheese

Combine first 5 ingredients in a small sauce pan cook over medium heat stirring constantly until butter melts. Cool to 105 degrees to 115 degrees. Dissolve yeast in warm water in a large bowl, let stand 5 minutes. Add milk mixture, eggs and 1 ½ cups flour, beat at low speed of electric mixer for 30 seconds. Beat at high speed 3 minutes stir in ½ cup parmesan cheese and enough remaining flour to make a stiff dough. Turn dough out onto a lightly floured surface. Knead until smooth and elastic (5 to 7 minutes) Place in a well greased bowl turning to grease top. Cover and let rise in a warm place 85 degrees free from drafts, 45 minutes or until doubled. Punch dough down let rest 10 minutes shape into 16 (2 inch) balls, dip the top of each in melted butter and coat with parmesan cheese. Arrange 8 rolls in each of 2 greased 9 inch cake pans. Cover and let rise in a warm place free from drafts until double in bulk. Bake at 375 degrees for 20 to 25 minutes. Makes 16 rolls.

Dilled Honey Wheat Rolls

1 package dry yeast
½ cup warm water (105 degrees to 115 degrees)
½ cup lite butter
1 (12 oz) carton lite cream style cottage cheese
3 tablespoons honey
1 tablespoon instant minced onion
2 teaspoon dill seeds
1 teaspoon light salt
¼ teaspoon baking soda
1 egg beaten
2 cups whole wheat flour
2 cups all purpose flour

Dissolve yeast in warm water let stand 5 minutes. Combine butter and cottage cheese in a large mixing bowl, stir well add yeast mixture and remaining ingredients except flour. Beat 1 minute on medium speed with an electric mixer. Gradually stir in flour to form a stiff dough. Turn dough out onto a lightly floured surface. Knead until smooth and elastic (5 to 7 minutes). Place in a well greased bowl, turning to grease top. Cover and let rise in a warm place (85 degrees) free from drafts 1 hour or until doubled in bulk. Punch dough down, shape into 24 (1 ½ inch) balls arrange in a greased 13x9x2 inch baking pan cover and let rise in a warm place free from drafts 45 minutes or until doubled. Bake at 400 degrees for 15 to 18 minutes. Makes 2 dozen.

Southern Corn Bread

1 egg beaten
1–1/3 cup 2% milk
¼ cup Canola oil

2 cups self rising corn meal mix
1–2 tablespoons splenda

Heat oven to 450 degrees. Grease 9 inch oven proof skillet or 9 inch square pan place in oven to heat. In large bowl combine all ingredients mix well. Pour batter into hot greased pan. Bake at 450 degrees for 20 to 25 minutes
5 to 8 servings

Old Fashion Southern Biscuits

1 package yeast
½ cup lukewarm water
5 cups all purpose flour
1 teaspoon baking soda
1 teaspoon salt
1 tablespoon baking powder
2 tablespoons splenda
¾ cup light butter
2 cups low fat buttermilk

Preheat oven to 400 degrees. Dissolve yeast in warm water; set aside. Mix dry ingredients together. Cut in butter. Add yeast and buttermilk and mix well. Turn dough onto lightly floured surface and roll out to desired thickness. Cut with small biscuit cutter and place on greased baking sheet. Bake for 12 minutes or until golden brown.

Mother's Rolls

½ cup light butter
¼ cup splenda
1 teaspoon light salt

½ cup boiling water
1 package yeast
½ cup lukewarm water
1 egg
3 cups sifted all purpose flour

Cream together light butter, splenda, and light salt. Add boiling water. Dissolve yeast in ½ cup lukewarm water; beat egg and add. Mix with flour. Beat well. Set aside at room temperature for 30 minutes, then refrigerate until needed. Preheat oven to 350 degrees. Roll out dough and cut into rolls. Place on greased cookie sheet. Bake for 15 minutes or until brown.

Buttery Biscuits Rolls

1 cup (2 sticks) light butter
1 cup light sour cream
2 cups self-rising flour

Preheat the oven to 350 degrees. Melt the butter in a large saucepan over medium low heat, whisk until completely melted. Add the sour cream and flour, and mix lightly. Spoon the batter into miniature muffin cups(do not grease) filling each one to the top. Bake for 15 minutes. Serve immediately (Note to freeze remove the rolls from the oven several minutes early. Cool completely before freezing. To serve thaw the rolls and bake at 350 degrees for only a few minutes until golden brown) Makes approximately 2 dozen.

Peanut Butter Bread

2 cups all purpose flour
1/3 cup splenda

1 teaspoon light salt
4 teaspoons baking powder
1 ½ cups milk
½ cup reduced fat peanut butter

Preheat oven to 375 degrees. Combine dry ingredients. Add milk and peanut butter. Pour into a greased 8x4x3 inch loaf pan. Bake for approximately 50 minutes. Great with jelly or jam.

Pineapple Cheese Bread

2 cups self-rising flour
¾ cup splenda
1 cup canned crushed pineapple with juice
2 eggs
2 tablespoons canola oil
¾ cup grated sharp 2% milk cheddar cheese
½ cup chopped walnuts
½ teaspoon pineapple extract

Preheat over to 350 degrees. Sift flour into a large mixing bowl and add splenda. Mix together. In a separate bowl, mix pineapple, eggs and oil and add to flour mixture, mixing well. Fold in cheese, nuts, and pineapple extract. Pour into a greased 9x3 inch loaf pan. Bake for 1 hour. Cool and turn out from pan, allowing to cool completely before slicing.

Muffins

Blueberry Muffins

1 ¾ cup all purpose flour
1/3 cup splenda
4 ½ teaspoons baking powder
½ teaspoon salt
1 cup fresh or frozen blueberries
¾ cup skim milk
1 egg
1/3 cup melted light butter

In a large bowl, combine flour, splenda, baking powder and salt. Stir in blueberries. Add skim milk, egg and light butter mix just until dry ingredients are moistened. The batter will be lumpy do not over beat. Spoon batter into twelve greased muffin cups. Bake at 400 degrees for 25 minutes or until tops spring back when lightly touched serve warm.
1 dozen

Pecan Muffins

2 cups all purpose flour
1 tablespoon baking soda
1 teaspoon ground cinnamon
¼ teaspoon salt
2 eggs
1 cup skim milk
¼ cup canola oil

½ teaspoon brown splenda
1 teaspoon vanilla extract

Topping
¼ cup light butter melted
¼ cup brown splenda
1 cup chopped pecans

In a large bowl combine flour, baking powder, cinnamon and salt. In another bowl, beat the eggs, milk, oil, brown splenda and vanilla until smooth. Stir into dry ingredients just until moistened. Into each greased muffin cup spoon batter, 1 teaspoon light butter, 1 teaspoon brown splenda and 1 heaping tablespoon of chopped nuts, top each with ¼ teaspoon of butter. Bake at 350 degrees for 25–30 minutes serve warm.
1 dozen

Chocolate Chip Muffins

2 ½ cups all purpose flour
1 ¼ cups quick cooking oats
1 cup splenda
2 ½ teaspoon baking soda
1 teaspoon salt
½ cup reduced fat peanut butter
1/3 cup canola oil
2 eggs
2 cups light buttermilk
4 ½ cups bran flakes
1 cup semisweet chocolate chips

In a bowl combine the flour, oats, splenda, baking soda and salt, set aside. In a large mixing bowl beat the peanut butter and oil until combined. Beat in the eggs and buttermilk. Stir into the dry ingredients just

until moistened. Fold in the cereal and chocolate chips. Fill greased muffin cups two thirds full. Bake at 400 degrees for 14–17 minutes. Cool for 5 minutes before removing from pans.
About 2 ½ dozen

Jam Filled Muffins

2 cups all purpose flour
½ cup splenda
1 tablespoon baking soda
½ teaspoon salt
2 eggs
2/3 cup skim milk
1/3 cup lite butter melted
½ cup sugar free strawberry preserves

In a large bowl combine flour and sugar. In a small bowl lightly beat eggs. Add milk and butter. Pour into dry ingredients and stir until moistened. Spoon half of the batter into 12 greased muffin cups. Make a well in the center of each. Add preserves. Spoon remaining batter over preserves. Bake at 400 degrees for 20–25 minutes
1 dozen

Oatmeal Raisin Muffins

1 cup quick cooking oats
1 ¼ cup buttermilk
1 egg lightly beaten
½ cup packed brown splenda
1/3 cup canola oil
2 cups all purpose flour
1 tablespoon baking soda

1 teaspoon salt
¼ teaspoon ground cinnamon
¼ teaspoon ground cloves
½ cup raisins

In a small bowl combine oats and buttermilk. In a small mixing bowl combine the egg, brown splenda and oil, stir in oat mixture. Combine the dry ingredients. Stir into batter just until moistened. Fold in raisins. Fill greased muffin cups. Bake at 400 degrees for 15–18 minutes. Cool for 5 minutes before removing from pan.
1 dozen

Apple Pumpkin Muffins

2 ½ cups all purpose flour
2 cups splenda
1 teaspoon baking soda
1 teaspoon ground cinnamon
½ teaspoon ground ginger
½ teaspoon salt
¼ teaspoon ground nutmeg
2 eggs
1 cup canned pumpkin
½ cup canola oil
2 cups finely chopped peeled tart apples

In a large bowl combine the first seven ingredients. In a small bowl, combine eggs, pumpkin and oil; stir into dry ingredients just until moistened. Fold in apples. Fill greased or paper lined muffins cups two-thirds full. Bake at 350 degrees for 30–35 minutes or until muffins test done. Cool for 10 minutes before removing from pan.
Yield 1 ½ dozen

Banana-Nut Muffins

½ cup light butter softened
1 cup splenda
2 large eggs
2 large ripe bananas mashed
2 cups all purpose flour
1 teaspoon salt
1 teaspoon baking powder
½ teaspoon baking soda
1 cup light buttermilk
½ cup chopped pecans
1 teaspoon vanilla extract

Beat together butter and splenda at medium speed until light and fluffy. Add eggs one at a time beating well after each addition. Beat in bananas until smooth. Mix together flour, salt, baking powder and baking soda. Alternately stir flour mixture and buttermilk into egg mixture until dry ingredients are just moistened. Stir in nuts and vanilla do not over mix. It should not be completely smooth. Spoon batter into prepared pans filling two-thirds full. Bake until lightly golden at 400 degrees.
Servings 12

Beverages

Limeade Cooler

¾ cup fresh lime juice (about 10 limes)
16 packets splenda
5 cups cold water
1 lime sliced

Squeeze limes over fine mesh strainer into measuring cup. Discard pulp. In a large pitcher, add lime juice, splenda and cold water. Stir in lime slices. Pour into chilled glasses and serve over ice.

Apple & Cranberry Tea

5 individual tea bags
5 cups boiling water
5 cups unsweetened apple juice
2 cups light cranberry juice
½ cup splenda
1/3 cup lemon juice
1 teaspoon cinnamon
¼ teaspoon cloves

Place the tea bags in a large heat proof bowl. Add boiling water cover and steep for 8 minutes. Discard tea bags. Add the remaining ingredients to tea, stir until splenda is dissolved. Serve warm or over ice
3 quarts.

Russian Tea

This is great in cold weather.

½ cup instant tea
2 ½ cup splenda
2 cups sugar free tang
1 teaspoon cloves
2 packs of kool aid unsweetened lemonade

Mix all ingredients store in an air tight container. Mix spoonfuls to taste in a cup of hot water.

Lemon & Lime Punch

1 (46 oz.) can pineapple juice
1 quart apple juice
1 liter diet bottle lemon lime carbonated beverage
1 (6 oz) can frozen lemonade concentrate, thawed and undiluted
1 orange sliced
1 lime sliced

Combine first 4 ingredients in a punch bowl. Add orange and lime slices serve over ice cubes
3 ½ quarts

Green Tea Punch

3 cups boiling water
6 green tea bags
2 teaspoons splenda
1 cup chilled cranberry juice

Brew tea bags in water 1 ½ minutes remove tea bags. Stir in splenda and chilled juice.

Southern Ice Tea

5 individual tea bags
5 cups boiling water
½ cup splenda
lemon juice optional

Place the tea bags in a large heat proof bowl. Add boiling water cover and steep for 8 minutes. Discard tea bags. Add splenda and stir until dissolved. Serve over ice
3 quarts.

Fruit Tea

5 individual tea bags
5 cups boiling water
½ cup splenda
½ cup orange juice
¼ cup lemon juice
¼ cup lime juice
¾ cup light cranberry juice

Place the tea bags in a large heat proof bowl. Add boiling water cover and steep for 8 minutes. Discard tea bags. Add the remaining ingredients to tea, stir until splenda is dissolved. Serve over ice.
3 quarts.

Successful Cooking Tips

1. Check the ingredients list.
2. Read the entire recipe from start to finish.
3. Set out all ingredients and equipment needed to prepare the recipes on the counter.
4. Do as much advance preparation as possible before actually cooking, chop, cut and grate.
5. Use a kitchen timer.
6. For best results follow the recipe instructions exactly.
7. Measure carefully. Use glass measures for liquids and metal or plastic cups for dry ingredients.
8. Clean up as you go.

A Note about Splenda

Splenda has been extensively tested and found to be safe, so we can all use it with confidence. If you want to reduce your sugar intake or calorie intake its for you. If you have diabetes its for you. What I like about Splenda is that it can help you follow a healthy diet because it provides the sweet taste of sugar without the calories and is ideal for cooking and baking. It can help all of us satisfy that desire for good tasting low calorie food and beverages.

About the Author

Frances Campbell is a life long resident of the small town of Calhoun, Georgia. She has been a member of Blackwood Springs Baptist Church for many years. She is retired from the Calhoun-Gordon County Childcare Center where she was a teacher. She has two children. She still resides in Calhoun, Georgia.

Index

Angel Rolls, 122
Apple & Cranberry Tea, 136
Apple Cake, 91
Apple Lettuce Salad, 18
Apple Pie, 79
Apple Pumpkin Muffins, 134
Applesauce Cake, 97
Applesauce Pork Loin, 58
Apricot Chicken, 49
Apricot Honey Chicken Poupon, 50
Asparagus Casserole, 36
Avanti's Grits, 45
Avocado Mandarin Salad, 17

Bacon Topped Meat Loaf, 62
Bacon Walnut Bread, 122
Baked Chicken Poupon, 50
Baked Mushroom Chicken, 53
Banana Bread, 120
Banana Oatmeal Cookies, 115
Banana Pops, 2
Banana Pudding, 85
Banana-Nut Muffins, 135
Beef Stew, 11
Beef Stroganoff, 66
Blueberry Muffins, 131
Blueberry Pudding, 86
Broccoli Casserole, 32

Broccoli Casserole, 34
Broccoli Mustard Sauce, 33
Brownies, 118
Brunswick Stew, 10
Buttery Biscuits Rolls, 129

Cabbage Casserole, 35
Caesar Salad, 24
Caramel Apple Cake with Caramel
    Topping, 104
Caramel Squares, 114
Caramelized Sugar Popcorn, 4
Carrot Bread, 120
Carrot Broccoli Casserole, 37
Carrot Cake, 98
Carrots and Pineapple, 31
Cashew Tossed Salad, 25
Catfish with Ginger Sauce, 72
Cheddar Broccoli Salad, 18
Cheese Biscuits, 125
Cheese Deviled Eggs, 6
Cheese Nibbler, 8
Cheese Sticks, 5
Cheesesteak Pasta, 65
Cheesy Chicken Rice Bake, 54
Cheesy Pineapple Casserole, 41
Cherry Pork Chops, 58
Cherry Waldorf Salad, 17

Chicken & Dumplings, 52
Chicken Livers and Bacon, 3
Chicken Rice Waldorf Salad, 21
Chicken Salad on Cantaloupe Rings, 24
Chicken Salad, 21
Chicken Soup, 15
Chicken Tarragon, 48
Chicken with Cherry Sauce, 53
Chicken with Sour Cream Gravy, 49
Chili, 13
Chinese Chicken Salad, 22
Chocolate Chip & Walnut Cookies, 111
Chocolate Chip Cake, 103
Chocolate Chip Cookies, 109
Chocolate Chip Muffins, 132
Chocolate Fruit Dip, 3
Chocolate Meringue Pie, 83
Chocolate Pie, 78
Chocolate Pound Cake, 101
Chocolate Ribbon Pie, 82
Cocoa Angel Food Cake, 90
Coconut Cake, 93
Coconut Cream Pie, 77
Coconut Macaroons, 116
Colorful Veggie Bake, 33
Corn Pudding, 40
Cranberry Spread, 4
Cream Cheese Spread, 2
Creamed Cabbage, 28
Creamy Beef Strips, 67
Crunchy Chicken Fingers, 55

Date Nut Bread, 121
Deviled Eggs, 1

Dilled Honey Wheat Rolls, 127
Do Nothing Cake, 102
Double Layer Pumpkin Pie, 80
Dried Apple Slices, 5
Drop Sugar Cookies, 112

Easy Cobbler, 88
Easy Dinner Rolls, 124
Easy Pumpkin Pie, 80

Finger Rolls, 125
Forgotten Cookies, 116
Fresh Blueberry Pie, 82
Fresh Fruit Dip, 1
Fresh Strawberry Pie, 78
Fried Green Tomatoes, 28
Fruit Salad, 27
Fruit Tea, 138
Fruited Chicken Salad, 20

Garden Chicken Salad, 19
Georgia Peach Pie, 84
German Chocolate Cake, 90
Glazed Baby Carrots, 42
Glazed Mixed Nuts, 6
Green Bean Casserole, 36
Green Tea Punch, 137
Grilled Salmon, 72
Grilled Sirloin Steak, 64

Ham 'n' Biscuits, 9
Herbed Roast Beef, 62
Herbed Tomatoes, 42
Holiday Sugar Free Gelatin Salad, 23

Hoppin John, 39
Hot Hominy Casserole, 43
Hot Vidalia Onion Dip, 7
Hummingbird Cake, 95

Ice Box Cookies, 115
Italian Dinner Rolls, 126

Jam Filled Muffins, 133

Lemon & Lime Teas, 137
Lemon Meringue Pie, 76
Lemon Sugar Cookies, 118
Limeade Cooler, 136
Low Fat Biscuits, 124

Macadamia Nut Cookies, 113
Macaroni and Cheese, 44
Maple Glazed Pork Chops, 59
Marinated Baked Chicken, 47
Mother's Rolls, 128
Mushroom Oven Rice, 37
Mushroom Soup, 15

Navy Bean Soup, 16
No Bake Banana Cream Pie, 81

Oatmeal Raisin Muffins, 133
Old Fashion Southern Biscuits, 128
Old Time Lemon Cheesecake, 106
Onion Soup, 13
Orange Pork Chops, 56
Oven French Fries, 30
Oven Fried Okra, 29

Oven Fried Zucchini Spears, 30

Parmesan Chicken, 48
Pastel Cookies, 117
Peanut Butter Apple Dip, 2
Peanut Butter Bread, 129
Peanut Butter Cookies, 110
Peanut Oatmeal Cookies, 111
Pecan Cookies, 110
Pecan Muffins, 131
Pecan Pie, 81
Peppercorn Steak, 63
Pineapple Cake, 105
Pineapple Cheese Bread, 130
Pineapple Upside Down Cake, 100
Pinto Beans, 39
Pork Chops & Apples, 57
Pork Chops Parmesan, 60
Pork Chops with Mustard Crumbs, 60
Pound Cake, 102

Quick Tuna Casserole, 74

Ranch Dip, 8
Raspberry Salad, 25
Red Velvet Cake, 99
Rice Pudding, 86
Roast Beef and Gravy, 64
Roasted Brussels Sprouts with Bacon, 34
Roasted Chicken, 47
Russian Tea, 137

Salad and Vinaigrette Dressing, 19
Salisbury Steak, 66

Saucy Turkey, 68
Sausage Balls, 3
Shrimp with Noodles, 71
Shrimp with Rice, 74
Sirloin Steak with Golden Onions, 65
Southern Corn Bread, 127
Southern Ice Tea, 138
Southern Jambalaya, 75
Southern Style Black-eye Peas, 38
Southern Tea Cakes, 113
Spice Cake, 96
Squash Casserole, 31
Stewed Salmon, 73
Strawberry Nut Salad, 23
Stuffed Apple Ring Salad, 26
Sweet Georgia Peanuts, 7
Sweet Potato Cake, 106
Sweet Potato Pie, 79
Sweet Potato Surprise, 45
Sweet Slaw, 43

Tarragon Salmon, 71
Tender Pork Chops, 57
Tender Pork Ribs, 56
Thanksgiving Dressing, 45
The Compromise Cake, 107

Thumb Print Cookies, 114
Tomato Soup, 14
Tuna Salad, 26
Turkey Apple Salad, 21
Turkey Bake, 69
Turkey Breast, 69
Turkey Meatloaf, 70
Turkey Vegetable Soup, 12
Turkey with Gravy, 68
Turnip Greens, 38

Vegetable Casserole, 32
Vegetable Ham Soup, 12
Vegetable Medley, 40
Vegetable Soup, 10
Vegetarian Soup, 14
Vidalia Onion Dip, 8

Walnut Apple Desert, 88
Walnut Chicken Skillet, 51
Whole Wheat Rolls, 123
Wrapped Garlic Chicken, 54

Yellow Cake, 92

Zucchini & Onion with Mozzarella, 41

978-0-595-41565-6
0-595-41565-2